THE
STOLEN
ELECTION

Hayes versus Tilden—1876

THE
STOLEN
ELECTION

---—◖◀(◍)▶◗—---

Hayes versus Tilden—1876

Lloyd Robinson

A TOM DOHERTY ASSOCIATES BOOK
NEW YORK

Contents

Foreword to the 2001 Edition   7

1   North Against South   13

2   Democrat Against Republican   35

3   Choosing the Candidates   53

4   Hayes Against Tilden   71

5   The Campaign Begins   97

6   The Nation Chooses   115

7   The Struggle for Votes   131

8   Who Counts the Votes?   143

9   The Electoral Commission   163

10   The End of the Crisis   185

11   The Aftermath   199

For Further Information   215

Index   217

Foreword to the 2001 Edition

I wrote this book in the summer of 1967, at a time of great domestic trouble in the United States. I wrote it partly because I wanted to retell a fascinating episode in American history, and partly because I suspected that, in the turbulent state of our nation back then, we might find ourselves living through some sort of replay of the Hayes-Tilden election someday. I stated this explicitly in the prophetic final paragraph of the book, and I will be giving away no surprises if I quote from that paragraph now:

> Probably we will be spared the turmoil and the agony of a disputed electoral count again, but the possibility remains alive. And if it comes to pass, the entire world will watch in fear and wonder as the giant of democracy struggles once more to choose its leader.

The national troubles of 1967 are matters for the historians now. The war that we were fighting in Southeast Asia, which so bitterly divided the country between those who thought we were defending a sacred trust and those who felt we were betraying the moral principles by which the United States has always claimed to live, eventually did come to an end. It left a legacy of political, social, and economic consequences, as wars always do, but, for better or for worse, our unhappy adventure in Vietnam has by this time ceased to be an active force in modern American life. And the other great issue of that time, that of providing full civil rights for the people who were then called Negroes, has also receded into the background of the national discourse. We are still a long way from true racial equality, of course. But we are no longer having a national debate over whether it was permissible to disqualify our black citizens from obtaining adequate housing, attending decent schools, holding mid- and upper-level jobs, or, for that matter, eating wherever they pleased and sitting wherever they pleased in public transportation, simply because they were black. It may now be hard to believe it, but all of those issues required direct legislative action in the 1960s before they were accepted as the law of the land in every one of the fifty states.

The divisions over Vietnam and civil rights in the 1960s raised the prospect of divided elections—the presence of third- and even fourth-party candidates who, unlike Ralph Nader and Patrick Buchanan in the 2000 election, might actually draw enough electoral votes away from the candidates of the major parties to throw an election into the House of Representatives for decision. As it turned out, no such thing happened. But Governor George C. Wallace of Alabama, the most outspoken Southern advocate of racial segregation, not only threatened such a third-party candidacy in 1967, but followed through on his threat and received 46 electoral votes in the Nixon-Humphrey election the following year. In a closer election, with an independent anti–Vietnam War candidate also on the ballots and drawing electoral votes, that might have been enough to require Congress to decide the outcome.

The political turmoil of the mid-1960s called to my mind the turmoil of the mid-1870s, when—with race the issue then, as it would be later—the complexities and structural inadequacies of our electoral system were laid bare by an excruciatingly close election that ultimately was decided, not by the American voters, but by a fifteen-member Electoral Commission consisting of five

Senators, five Representatives, and five Justices of the Supreme Court. From the distance of a century and a quarter, it is quite clear that the victory in the election of 1876 was stolen from the winning candidate, the Democrat Samuel J. Tilden, by fraudulent manipulations in four Southern states that were confirmed by a strictly partisan vote of this Electoral Commission.

After the troubled election of 1876, certain legislative reforms were put into place that supposedly would prevent a repetition of the Hayes-Tilden charade. But as we saw to our great dismay in November and December of 2000, our electoral system is still ridden with chasms of contradiction and the potential for chaos.

I do not happen to believe that the Bush-Gore election of 2000 was a "stolen" one in the Hayes-Tilden sense. It was certainly a hotly disputed one, but the dispute centered on methods of counting votes in one state, and—as the final 5–4 Supreme Court decision showed—the outcome depended, finally, on the interpretation of existing state law, rather than (as in 1876) the illegitimate overturning of properly conducted vote-counts by corrupt boards of local officials.

But that is not the point. What we all came to see, during the chaotic post-election weeks of 2000, is that chaos lurks behind the surface of the rules in any closely contested presidential election. Suppose Florida had not managed to certify any legitimate slate of electors in time for the meeting of the Electoral College: how many electoral votes, then, would it take to decide a winner? Would it be a majority among the remaining qualified electors—in which case Al Gore would have been elected—or a majority of the entire Electoral College, in which case, with neither candidate getting the requisite 270 votes, the House of Representatives would have had to decide? The Constitution does not clearly say. Other ambiguities also surfaced concerning the relative electoral roles of the House of Representatives and the Senate (whose presiding officer, permitted to cast a tie-breaking vote, was none other than Al Gore), and the power of the Florida state legislature, and of the Governor of Florida. Wherever one looked, one saw irreconcilable contradictions and mysteries in the deepest layers of our electoral law.

In the end, the United States Supreme Court cut through the chaos by terminating the tortured Florida vote-counting process before it became necessary to explore the deeper mysteries of our election law. The Court feared, I think rightly, that if the election were permitted to move on into Congress for a decision, the country might stumble on and on into confusion and division until, ultimately, the whole affair would return once again to the Supreme Court, but only after intolerable damage had been done. The Court's decision was a damage-control intervention.

In the aftermath of Bush-Gore has come a cry for reform of the system, just as there was in the aftermath of Hayes-Tilden. No doubt some changes will be made, though not, I think, anything as major as the abolition of the Electoral College itself and direct election of the President by popular vote. The basic system will probably survive. But certainly the lesson of Bush-Gore is that if an election contest is ever allowed to proceed into the farthest reaches of all the contingencies, we will quickly reach a point where various elements of the law butt up against each other in hopelessly contradictory fashion; and those built-in contradictions need to be fixed before the next election. I hope that they are.

Meanwhile, here is my account of the Hayes-Tilden fracas of 1876—as relevant, alas, as ever.

—LLOYD ROBINSON
January 2001

THE
STOLEN
ELECTION

Hayes versus Tilden—1876

1

North Against South

Nearly everyone knows the names of our first few Presidents: Washington, Adams, Jefferson, Madison, Monroe, those dignified and remote figures who took part in the birth of the United States. And the names of our recent Presidents are familiar, too: Roosevelt, Truman, Eisenhower, Kennedy. But some of the men who have occupied the White House are anything but vivid to us. It is hard to think of much to say about the Presidents who lived just before the Civil War, for example: Taylor, Fillmore, Pierce, Buchanan. And there is that other group of Chief Executives from the late nineteenth century who tend to blur into vagueness for us: Tilden, Arthur, Benjamin Harrison, Garfield—

Tilden?

Of course. Samuel Jones Tilden (1814–1886), the nineteenth President of the United States, elected on November 7, 1876, as the candidate of the Democratic Party to succeed the outgoing President Ulysses S. Grant.

The name seems even less familiar than others of its period. The words "President" and "Tilden" do not go naturally together, as they do for President Arthur, President Garfield, President Harrison, and the rest. And there is a good reason for that. Samuel J. Tilden was never sworn in as President of the United States. He was never inaugurated. He never resided in the White House or signed a single bill into law. In fact, although he won the election, he never became President, and was forced to stand by helplessly while the man he defeated, Rutherford B. Hayes, took possession of the nation's highest office.

Tilden was the victim of the greatest fraud in American political history. He received a quarter of a million more votes than his opponent. That in itself would not make a man President, for in our double system of voting we choose, not a Presidential candidate, but an Electoral College that meets to select the winner of the election. A man may lead in the popular vote and still not be chosen by the Electoral College. But Tilden also received a clear majority of the Electoral College—at least, when the first votes came in.

Nevertheless, he did not win. On the night of the election, Hayes and the Republicans went to bed thinking they had been beaten; Tilden and the Democrats celebrated their victory. In the morning, though, schemes were hatched and hurried conferences were held, and the process of reversing the decision of the voters got under way. That process dragged on for months, while the leaders of the nation debated and the citizens looked on in dismay and wonder. Election returns were thrown out by special committees. The votes of certain states were taken away from the Democrats and given to the Republicans. Confusion followed upon confusion. Both sides engaged in bribery, lawlessness, and trickery. The clock ticked out the final hours of President Grant's term of office, and still there was no one to take his place. Who would be President? What would happen to the country if Grant's term ended and no new President had been chosen? Would a second Civil War break out? Would there be a dictatorship? Would the Constitution collapse?

At the last moment the crisis was settled. The Republican, Hayes, took the Presidential oath. Some 30,000 Americans cheered the new President at his inauguration on March 5, 1877. Meanwhile other thousands of Americans sent letters and telegrams to Samuel J. Tilden, telling him that they still believed him to be the true President and urging him to seize power in the land. But Tilden accepted the verdict that had been forced on him. He could have fought the decision and perhaps split the nation by civil war, but he did not. Though privately convinced he should have been President, he told his supporters to give their allegiance to Hayes. And so the strangest and most controversial of American elections came to its end. The United States had survived a great crisis; it had shown that even in such a bizarre contest the result could be an orderly and peaceful transfer of power.

How could such an election have come about, though? How could a winner be transformed into a loser, and a loser into a winner? What were the circumstances that produced so unique a situation? And—was it really unique? Could something like the Hayes-Tilden election ever happen here again? Or is the stolen election of 1876 merely a chapter out of our picturesque past, something that now appears quaint and funny, an event from a distant era when it did not matter very much at all who was President of the United States?

Some of these questions can be answered easily. We know the means by which the presidency was taken away from Tilden and awarded to Hayes. We know something about the secret deals that brought this result about. We understand the forces that made the fraud possible.

But we cannot be certain that something like it will never happen again. Many of the angers and hatreds that turned the Election of 1876 into the Compromise of 1877 are still loose in our land—in somewhat different forms, true, but they still exist. Nor has there been any basic change in the way we elect our Presidents—a method which has several dangerous flaws. Most of the time, the system works smoothly and well; but on a few occasions in our past it has broken down, never more disastrously than in

1876. What happened then may one day have an ugly encore and send a shock wave of chaos rippling through the world—although we tell ourselves that it is not very likely.

Rutherford B. Hayes was a solemn but good-natured man, a hard worker, a loving husband and father, a capable public servant. He had fought and had been wounded in the Civil War; he had been elected to Congress and had been Governor of Ohio three times; he was honest, handsome, and sincere. He was popular among the citizens and he had no enemies among the professional politicians. He was the sort of man of whom it is often said that he was born to be President. Yet the voters did not elect him.

Samuel J. Tilden was an icy, aloof man with a forbidding manner and no fondness for public life. He was a bachelor. He had not taken any part in the Civil War; he was unimpressive physically; his health was poor. He had amassed millions of dollars through his cleverness as a lawyer. His cold, penetrating intellect was so brilliant that he made his own friends uncomfortable. He was a New Yorker, and the rest of the country tends to be suspicious of New Yorkers, especially if they are wealthy and brilliant. (Hayes was from Ohio, the heart of the land.) Tilden did not have the personal magnetism a successful candidate must have to win the support of the people, and professional politicians of both parties hated him because he had exposed their thievery. Yet the voters elected him President.

So it was not a contest of personalities. If it had been, Hayes would have won in a landslide. But in those days before radio and television, the personalities of the candidates did not matter much to the voters. The candidates stayed on their own front porches, making few speeches and never going on a campaign tour. The voters made their decisions on the basis of ideas and issues—not on how a man looked or how warmly he smiled.

The main issue of 1876 was North versus South.

That may sound a little strange. North versus South was the issue of 1860, after all. When Abraham Lincoln won the election that year—the first candidate of the Republican Party to become President—a group of southern states broke away from the Union. The leaders of the South feared that the new President would attempt to put an end to slavery; and so the South declared itself to be an independent nation, the Confederate States of America, where the white man would always have the right to make a slave of the black man. The North refused to allow such a nation to come into being. The bitter war of 1861–65 followed—America's greatest tragedy, with brother fighting against brother on American soil.

The powerful industrial North triumphed over the weak rural South. By the spring of 1865 the war was over. Slavery was abolished in the United States. The South, devastated by invasion and famine, was in ruins. The Confederacy was dead. Now was the time for the healing of the nation's wounds, for the joining of South to North once more. President Lincoln faced the problem of bringing the seceding states back into the Union and making them full partners in America again. It was a difficult task, calling for equal measures of forgiveness and sternness; but the warm, great-hearted Lincoln hoped that he could create harmony and win the allegiance of all Americans, Northerners and Southerners, white men and black.

He never got the chance. An assassin's bullet took his life just at the moment of victory. As the reunited nation faced the terrible challenges of peacetime, it found itself led by a new man, one who had never been meant to be President. And in the mistakes and confusions of the months just after the Civil War were planted the seeds of the conflict of 1876. The Hayes-Tilden election was actually the final act of the tragedy that had begun in 1860. One of the strangest aspects of this strange election is that the wrong man turned out to be the right man: Hayes, who should not have been President, brought the agonizing struggle of North against South to a close, which Tilden probably could not have done.

To understand what happened in 1876, we have to go back to April 14, 1865—less than a week after the end of the Civil War. President Lincoln, that night, went to Ford's Theater in Washington. An unemployed southern actor by the name of John Wilkes Booth, who hated Lincoln for freeing the slaves, stepped into the President's box and fired a single shot. By morning, Andrew Johnson of Tennessee was President.

Only weeks before his death, Lincoln had declared, "With malice toward none; with charity for all . . . let us strive . . . to bind up the nation's wounds." Now it was Johnson's assignment to bind those wounds, but Johnson was not the great man Lincoln had been. Lincoln had picked him to run for Vice-President in 1864 because he was a rarity, a Southerner who opposed slavery and supported the North in the Civil War. Johnson, a rough, poorly educated man from the Tennessee hills, had been Senator from Tennessee until it seceded from the Union, and later had been its military governor when it was conquered by the North. He did not even belong to the same political party as Lincoln, for Johnson was a Democrat. As a step toward national unity, Lincoln had tried to bring together the Republicans and the anti-slavery Democrats into a new party, the Union Party. This step was not entirely popular with Lincoln's fellow Republicans. When Lincoln said he would like Andrew Johnson to run with him, the fiery Representative Thaddeus Stevens of Pennsylvania, the most powerful Republican in Congress, grumbled, "Can't you get a candidate for Vice-President without going down into a damned rebel province for one?"

Now the "damned rebel" Johnson was in the White House.

The men of the North, who had fought and won a war to keep the Union free, wondered what the new President's policy toward the defeated South would be. His past record was good. He had been the only senator from a Confederate state to remain loyal to the Union, even though he had been driven into exile when Tennessee seceded. All during the war he had backed the North against his native South. Would he now continue to be tough with the seceders? Or would he try to win favor in the South by showing mercy?

A strong faction of Republicans, headed by Thad Stevens, had no sympathy at all for the defeated South. "Humble the proud traitors," Stevens declared. He wanted the South treated as a conquered province that the North could rule as it saw fit. Divide up the great plantations of the rebels, said Stevens, and sell the land at low prices to ex-slaves. Allow the freed slaves to vote and to run for public office. Take all political power away from the white aristocracy of the South, and hang the leaders of the secession. Those who agreed with the harsh, unforgiving Stevens were known as Radical Republicans. They meant to make sure that the southern whites knew the South had lost the war. The Radical Republicans had another motive, too: they expected that all the new Negro voters in the South would vote Republican, since the Democratic Party was the party of the slaveowners. Thus, bolstered by the votes of hundreds of thousands of former slaves, the Republicans would remain in power indefinitely.

But Andrew Johnson, as President, turned out to be mild in his treatment of the South. He tried to guide himself by Lincoln's words and to show malice toward none, charity for all. Acting in what he thought were the best interests of the entire nation, President Johnson proclaimed a general pardon for most of the Confederate soldiers and refused to execute the rebel leaders. Under his program of "Restoration," he took no action to confiscate rebel property, to take away the citizenship of those who had seceded, or to grant equal rights to the Negroes. He wanted to move gradually on the question of letting ex-slaves vote and hold office, hoping that time would end the bitterness between white and black in the South. He planned to let the eleven Confederate states back into the Union with their old white leaders still in control. In August 1866 President Johnson announced, not very realistically, that "peace, order, tranquality, and civil authority now exist in and throughout the whole of the United States."

He was wrong. In the South, the whites who had been restored to power were quick to take advantage of their unexpected good fortune. They passed "Black Laws" forcing the freed slaves to accept wages and working conditions imposed by their old owners, and forbidding them from exercising the rights of free men. Northerners were horrified. It looked as though President Johnson had canceled the effects of the Civil War overnight, by letting the losers live much as they had lived before. Such newspapers as the Chicago *Tribune* denounced the Black Laws, declaring, "We tell the white men of Mississippi that the men of the North will convert the State of Mississippi into a frog pond before they will allow any such laws to disgrace one foot of soil in which the bones of our soldiers sleep and over which the flag of freedom waves."

The Radical Republicans in particular were horrified by Johnson's "treason." It shocked them that the white Southerners were not being made to pay a heavy price for their rebellion. And they feared that soon the restored southern states would be sending so many Democratic Representatives and Senators to Washington that Republican power would be broken. The bitter, vindictive Thad Stevens goaded the Radical Republicans into action.

When Congress met late in 1865, the Radicals pushed through a ruling that no Congressmen-elect from the former Confederate states would be allowed to take their seats until there had been a full investigation. A committee of fifteen was appointed to investigate—with Thad Stevens as its chairman. Naturally, none of the Southerners were allowed into Congress. That took care of the immediate threat to Radical control.

Next, Congress forced through two bills granting citizenship and civil rights to Negroes. These measures were designed to cope with the Black Laws of the South. They would not have permitted Negroes to vote—even in the North most Negroes were not allowed to cast ballots then—but otherwise they would serve to protect black men against white abuse. The President vetoed both bills. One was passed over his veto and became law; the other died.

Then the Radicals proposed the Fourteenth Amendment to the Constitution, which was designed to give Negroes the vote. It prohibited the states from depriving "any person of life, liberty, or property, without due process of law," and established penalties on those states that denied some of their citizens the right to vote. The Fourteenth Amendment also prevented anyone from holding public office who had previously taken an oath to support the Constitution of the United States and then had "engaged in insurrection or rebellion against the same, or given aid or comfort to the enemies thereof." Since nearly every southern official of pre–Civil War days, from state legislators up to members of Congress, had taken oaths to support the Constitution, this clause effectively eliminated all those prewar leaders from an active role in political life. The Amendment specified that the restriction could be removed only by a two-thirds vote of Congress.

The southern states were not allowed to send Representatives or Senators to Congress unless they ratified the Fourteenth Amendment. Only Tennessee voted to ratify in 1866. The others preferred to withhold civil rights from Negroes even if it meant losing a voice in Congress. But the Radicals were not through punishing the South. In May 1866, southern whites rioted at Memphis, Tennessee, and many Negroes were killed. An even bloodier riot in New Orleans two months later took the lives of more than two hundred black men. Thaddeus Stevens used these riots as evidence that the South would go on oppressing the ex-slaves unless strong measures were taken. He called for voters to elect a Congress dominated by Radical Republicans in November.

President Johnson was not running the office himself in 1866. In September, though, he went on what was called "a swing around the circle"—a campaign tour that took him from Washington to Chicago and back by way of such important cities as Philadelphia, New York, Cleveland, Detroit, St. Louis, and Pittsburgh. Wherever he went, he delivered speeches asking tolerance for the defeated South. But hecklers with Radical beliefs jeered and howled at him. He lost his temper, and shouted back, which only led people to think that the President was a rash and foolish man. In the elections the Radical Republicans kept control of Congress.

Because ten of the eleven southern states had refused to ratify the Fourteenth Amendment, the Radicals claimed that it was necessary for Congress to take swift action to protect the rights of the former slaves. On March 2, 1867, Congress passed the first Reconstruction Act, which stripped the white Southerners of the power Johnson had given them. The state governments created in 1865–66 were abolished and the ten southern states were divided into five military districts, each ruled by a major general of the United States Army. Twenty thousand troops were sent into the South to maintain order. The Black Laws were thrown out and the South was compelled to accept the Fourteenth Amendment. Some 700,000 Negroes, most of them unable to read and write, were allowed to vote in the southern states. Thousands of whites were disqualified from voting because they had supported the

Confederacy. By the time the Radicals got through rearranging the voting lists, only about 627,000 whites in the South had the right to vote. They were outnumbered by the votes of their former slaves.

It amounted to a revolution. In one stroke, the Radicals took the South away from the white masters and gave it to the slaves. Gone was the spirit of gradual change; gone was forgiveness, gone was toleration. What the whites had done to the Negroes was serious enough, but Radical Reconstruction in the South was just as severe a misuse of power. Over the objections of the helpless President Johnson, the Radicals set up a military dictatorship in the South and proceeded to mete out vengeance to their foes.

New elections were held there. Hundreds of thousands of ex-slaves, hardly believing that all this could be true, went to the polls and voted. One state, South Carolina, elected a legislature in which Negroes actually had an 87-to-69 majority over whites. In the other nine states there were many new Negro legislators, though they were not in the majority. The whites who were elected were not the old slaveowners, either. They were ambitious, unscrupulous men who were willing to cooperate with the Radical Republicans because they hoped to get rich at public expense. Some of these men were native Southerners, who became known as scalawags because they were regarded as traitors to their homeland. Others were from the North; they had hurriedly packed their bags and rushed South in search of power and money. They were called carpetbaggers. Now the secessionist states were finally permitted to come back into the Senate and the House of Representatives. But the new southern members of Congress were carpetbaggers and scalawags. They were Republicans, and not all of them were white. The old Democratic southern white aristocracy had been frozen out.

In practice the Negroes had very little to say about the way the ten reconstructed states were ruled. Giving people the vote is not the same thing as giving them an understanding of how to govern; and it is hard for people unable to read and write to pass laws. Though there were some Negro leaders of great ability, most of the ex-slaves were content to let the scalawags and carpetbaggers run the show on their behalf. So the South was still dominated by whites, after all. Few Negroes were elected to the highest offices during Reconstruction. None became the governor of a state. Two Negroes from Mississippi served in the United States Senate, and fourteen Negroes were elected to the House of Representatives, six of them from South Carolina. Mississippi had a Negro lieutenant governor, secretary of state, superintendent of public education, and treasurer; South Carolina had five high Negro officials, including an associate justice of the state supreme court. None of this would have been possible before the war. But the real rulers of the South were the Radical Republican white carpetbaggers and scalawags. They told the Negroes which candidates to vote for, and the Negroes generally did as they were told.

Naturally, the Radicals did a great deal for their Negro supporters. South Carolina passed a law making it illegal to call a man a "nigger" in that state. New schools were opened for Negroes; special courts were established to hear their grievances against their white masters. Decades of neglect were atoned for with progressive and important measures. On the other hand, not all the programs of the Reconstructionists were noble ones. The carpetbagger-dominated legislatures imposed heavy taxes against the rich white landowners and pocketed much of the money that was raised. They confiscated land and property, dividing it among themselves. The defeated Confederates were victimized and tyrannized for the profit of their new masters.

Since the southern whites could not fight back legally by voting for men they could support, they fought back illegally. They organized terrorist groups like the Ku Klux Klan, and rode about the countryside at night in white robes and masks, beating and killing Negroes. Through whippings, threats, and murders they forced many frightened blacks to stay "in line," and not to take advantage of the opportunities offered by Reconstruction. The northern Radicals met force with force and sent more troops into the South. It began to look as though the country was entering a prolonged period of strife in which the Union victory in the Civil War could be preserved only by a permanent military occupation of the South.

When President Johnson tried to defy the Radicals, they impeached him—the only time this has happened to an American President. He was brought to trial in 1868 on eleven charges of "high crimes and misdemeanors," and only by a single vote was spared from losing his office. His term was almost over by then, and he knew he had no chance to win the election in November, or even to be nominated. The Republicans nominated the hero of the Civil War, General Ulysses S. Grant, and he won an easy victory over his Democratic opponent, Horatio Seymour of New York.

Grant was a short, round-shouldered man with a straggly beard and a modest, humble manner. Before the war he had been a failure at everything he attempted: he was unsuccessful in business and won no reputation in the peacetime army, and in the 1850s he was so short of cash that he tried to sell his wife's two Negro slaves to have money to live on. In the war, though, Grant demonstrated unexpected brilliance and courage as a general, and led the Union to triumph. He had never been active in politics—in fact, had never even bothered to vote—but the Republicans saw that he could win the election, and they were right. Without the votes of 700,000 Negroes, though, he might have lost—especially if all the white Democrats of the South had been allowed to vote.

The South remained Republican during Grant's first term, be-cause government troops were there to keep the carpetbaggers and scalawags in power. But the unpopular Reconstructionists had only a weak grip on the southern states, and not even the soldiers could strengthen it indefinitely. The white South talked of "redemption"—meaning the return of the ten states to white Democratic rule. The Ku Klux Klan terrifed many Negroes away from the polls; the greed of the carpetbaggers aroused anger among many neutral citizens; and, one by one, the southern states were "redeemed" through elections. The Democrats won control of Virginia and North Carolina in 1870 and of Georgia in 1871, and they looked forward to the redemption of the other recon-structed states.

The weakness of Grant as President helped their cause. Grant was an innocent, trusting man who depended heavily on friends for advice—and some of his friends were conniving, corrupt poli-ticians. Bribery and graft became common in Washington. Grant's Secretary of the Navy, George M. Robeson, banked $320,000 in four years by taking illegal fees from contractors. Railroad tycoons showered Congressmen and cabinet members with millions of dollars in return for special privileges. Grant knew nothing of what was going on; he surrounded himself with cronies who took good care to shield him from the truth. The Republican Party began to split apart as a result of the general corruption. It broke into two factions—the "Liberal Republi-cans," who wanted reform, and the "Stalwarts," who were get-ting rich on graft and wanted things to stay pretty much as they were.

In 1872 the Liberal Republicans decided to oppose the re-elec-tion of Grant. They did not blame him personally for the atmo-sphere of scandal in the government, nor did they accuse him of taking part in the frauds and thefts. But they felt that a new man should have the presidency and sweep away the grafters. To run on a special Liberal Republican ticket they nominated Horace Greeley, editor of the New York *Tribune*—an elderly, tender-hearted man who disliked the Radicals and favored reconciliation with the South. The Democrats also nominated Greeley. The Stalwart Republicans, though, put Grant up for office again.

Despite all the evidence of crookedness in his administration, Grant was re-elected, but it was far from an honorable victory. The campaign against Greeley was so vicious and insulting that his health broke under the cruel ridicule. He was accusing of wanting to give the South back to the slaveowners, and that was enough to let Grant carry all of the northern states. Grant carried most of the carpetbag South, too, because government troops were standing by to make sure that the people voted Republican. The troops, veterans of the Civil War, were loyal to Grant and the Republicans, and kept many white Democrats away from the polls while letting black Republicans vote. In Texas and Georgia, where the troops had been withdrawn, Greeley was the winner. He also carried the border states of Missouri, Kentucky, Maryland, and Tennessee.

The voting in Louisiana was marked by the worst frauds of all. Louisiana had not yet been "redeemed" and was occupied by United States troops, but a complicated political situation had developed there in 1872. Henry C. Warmoth, the carpetbagger Republican governor elected four years earlier, had quarreled with his own party and had changed sides. Now he was supporting the Democratic candidate to succeed him, John McEnery. The Republicans had named a radical, William P. Kellogg, to run for governor as the only white man on a ticket that included six Negroes. In the voting, Louisiana's large Negro population naturally chose the Kellogg ticket, while the whites voted for the Democrat McEnery. It is hard to say which side really won; but Governor

Warmoth had his own appointees count the votes, and they announced that the Democrats had triumphed. According to Warmoth, the Democrats had captured the governorship and the legislature of Louisiana and they had given the state's presidential vote to Greeley.

The Republicans took the issue to court. They got a Federal judge, who had been appointed to office by Grant, to order a new count of the votes. The judge prohibited the Democratic-controlled legislature from meeting, and appointed a Republican-controlled board to check the ballots. Naturally, the recount showed that the Republicans had carried Louisiana. But the Democrats refused to accept this decision. While Kellogg was installed as Governor of Louisiana with the help of Federal soldiers' bayonets, the Democrats set up a rival government under McEnery. There were two governors and two legislatures—one carpetbagger-run, one Democrat-run. And each side's election board sent its own set of returns in the Presidential voting to Washington.

Congress was called upon to decide which set of Louisiana returns to accept. It solved the puzzle in the simplest way, by throwing out both. That year it did not matter, since the national election had not been close. But the double returns from Louisiana were an ominous sign for the future. When the same thing happened four years later, no easy solution was available.

Greeley, who had lost the election, his sick wife, and his newspaper all within one month, sank into a final and fatal illness soon afterward. "We have been terribly beaten," he said. "I was assailed so bitterly that I hardly knew whether I was running for the presidency or the penitentiary." Four weeks after the election he was dead, and the Liberal Republican movement died with him.

The reformers had accomplished at least one thing, though. They had helped to weaken the carpetbaggers by giving the South back its prewar leadership. In May 1872, Congress had passed a law under Liberal Republican pressure that restored the right of office-holding to most of those who had been disqualified by the Fourteenth Amendment. Only a few hundred old Confederates, out of thousands, were not pardoned at this time. The others now were free to run for state and local offices and for Congress. The South's most distinguished white citizens emerged from forced retirement, and redemption seemed closer than ever for those states still under the domination of the carpetbaggers.

There was more trouble for the Stalwarts early in 1873. Grant's second term had just begun when the banking firm of Jay Cooke & Company went bankrupt. Cooke was the nation's most important banker, and a close friend of President Grant. Cooke's huge fortune had been freely at the disposal of the Republican Party. But he overextended himself in trying to promote the Northern Pacific Railroad, and when his bank failed it was a mighty embarrassment for the Republicans. More than that: his collapse led to the bankruptcy of others, and as the crisis grew thousands of businesses had to shut up shop in the summer of 1873. By September, the nation was plunged into full-scale financial panic. Hard times had come; millions were out of work and hungry. Now the reformers could say that Republican chicanery and graft had brought a disaster upon the country.

The Grant Administration was tremendously unpopular in 1874. In the North, the Republicans were disliked because of the financial panic; in the South, they were hated as always for the sins of the carpetbaggers. Those southern states that were still held down by garrisons of Federal troops began to stir restlessly and dream of redemption. A state election in Texas in December of 1873 resulted in overwhelming defeat for the Republican candidates. In Arkansas, a Republican governor, Baxter, had been elected with military help in 1872. In the spring of 1874, his defeated rival, Brooks, persuaded a state court to reverse the 1872 election. Brooks ejected Baxter by force from the state capitol. Both sides took up arms, and for a month Arkansas seemed ready to break into battle. Then the Federal government ordered the Republican, Baxter, returned to office. Brooks yielded, but the Arkansas Democrats were more eager than ever now to free themselves from Republican rule.

In Louisiana, two governments had been ruling since the beginning of 1873. The carpetbagger Kellogg was the official governor, but the white citizens ignored him and recognized the Democrat, McEnery, as governor. They organized a secret group called the White League, similar to the Ku Klux Klan, and plotted a revolution in Louisiana. On September 14, 1874, the White League rose in rebellion and overthrew the Kellogg government, after a battle in the streets of New Orleans in which sixteen whites and eleven Negroes were killed. Kellogg fled and McEnery moved into the state capitol.

The national government could hardly tolerate this. Whether or not Kellogg's election had been legitimate, he was now the legal governor, and to overthrow him by force was anarchy—the breakdown of all law. Grant ordered Federal troops to crush the White League and restore Kellogg to office. At gunpoint, the Democrats yielded. But only the presence of troops kept matters from turning into open war. Louisiana tottered on the brink of chaos. Leaders on both sides were kidnapped and murdered. Gangs clashed in the streets. Finally the violence grew so serious that a compromise was reached: the Democrats agreed to accept Kellogg as governor, provided the Democratic-controlled legislature was recognized as official. That calmed things down, although with a Republican governor and a Democratic legislature it was almost impossible for the state government of Louisiana to get anything done.

The situation was grim for the Grant Administration as the 1874 Congressional elections approached. Rightly or wrongly, the Republicans were blamed for the Panic of 1873 and for the unrest in the South, and they suffered for it in the voting. In the national elections, the Democrats took control of the House of Representatives with a majority of about 70. This was the first time that either house of Congress had been in Democratic power since the secession of the South in 1861. On the local level, the Democrats were also successful, defeating Republican governors and legislators everywhere, both in North and South. The Democrats redeemed the states of Alabama, Arkansas, and Texas in 1874, and went beyond that to capture control of such normally Republican northern states as Pennsylvania, Ohio, Indiana, and Massachusetts. Even the United States Senate, thought to be a safe Republican stronghold, nearly went to the Democrats. At that time the Senate was not elected by direct vote of the people; senators were chosen by the state legislatures. A state with a Democratic majority in its legislature would elect a Democratic senator, and so the newly installed Democratic legislators around the nation quickly replaced Republicans with Democrats in the Senate. Although the new Senate still had a Republican majority, it no longer had the two-thirds majority that was vital to complete control. With the House of Representatives now run by Democrats and the Senate only barely Republican, great changes were in store.

The chief loser in the 1874 election, it quickly appeared, was the American Negro. The Republicans were the party of Reconstruction, and had fought hard for Negro rights. Some Republicans were genuine idealists who believed in helping the long-exploited Negro. Others, more cynical, knew that showing sympathy for the ex-slaves would bring them Negro votes. The Democrats regarded every Negro as a potential Republican, and thus a political enemy. Both in the North and, of course, the South, Democrats worked to deprive the Negroes of their newly won votes. A typical Democratic attitude was expressed by Senator Thomas A. Hendricks of Indiana:

"I say that we are not of the same race; we are so different that we ought not to compose one political community. . . . I say . . . this is a white man's Government, made by the white man for the white man. . . . I am not in favor of giving the colored man a vote, because I think we should remain a political community of white people. I do not think it is for the good of either race that we should attempt to make the Government a mixed government of white and black. . . ."

The Republicans had made a campaign issue out of racial prejudice since 1866. They pointed to southern abuses of the Negro and appealed to honorable white men to vote Republican. This tactic was known as "waving the bloody shirt." Republicans waved the bloody shirt every time a Negro was lynched by the Ku Klux Klan, claiming that such crimes proved that the Democrats of the South were unfit to rule.

This approach had worked well in 1866, when the North had just finished fighting a dreadful and costly war for the sake of liberating the Negro. But accusations of southern bigotry no longer could help the Republicans in 1874. The white voters were tired of seeing the bloody shirt waved, tired of hearing about the downtrodden Negroes. The mood that year, in the aftermath of the Panic of 1873, was one of letting the Negroes shift for themselves; just then it seemed important to vote against the Republicans regardless of the race issue. And so the great Democratic victories of 1874 came about.

The day of the Radical Republicans was nearly over. The South was starting to escape from the torments of Reconstruction; the Democrats were emerging once again as a major national power;

the decade of unchallenged Republican rule was closing. So long as the North voted Republican and Federal troops throttled the Democrats of the South, Grant and his cronies were safe. But now the North had gone Democratic and the South was nearly rid of the corrupt, incompetent carpetbaggers who had plundered it so long. As 1874 drew to its close, the future looked melancholy for the Republicans. The following March, the new Congress would come to Washington to meet for the first time—a Congress with a host of unfamiliar Democratic faces. Surely there would be trouble from them. And nearly two years ahead lay a more serious crisis: the presidential election of 1876, when the entire Republican Party would be called to account by the nation for the way it had governed since the close of the Civil War.

2

Democrat Against Republican

The conflict in the nation was a clash of sections, a clash of ideas, and a clash of political parties. As today, the differences between the Republicans and the Democrats were not immensely great, but differences existed. And, as today, both the Democrats and the Republicans were split into bitter factions.

The Democrats were the older party. They went back to the early days of the United States, although at first they were known as Democratic Republicans. The Democrats took their modern form in the 1830s under the leadership of Andrew Jackson. They were a divided party even then, because they included two groups of differing interests—the rich slaveowners of the South and the poorly paid workers of the big northern cities. In many ways these early Democrats were liberal and progressive, eager to do things for the ordinary citizen of low income. But there was always that element of conservative slaveowners exerting influence in the southern branch of the party.

Before the Civil War the chief opponents of the Democrats were known as the Whigs. They included all those who disliked a strong central government. While farmers, laborers, and shopkeepers tended to join the Democrats, the Whigs drew their support from bankers, stockbrokers, and manufacturers. Men of property, men of business, backed the Whigs. Most Whigs were quite satisfied with the state of society as it then existed, and did not want the government to interfere by doing such things as taxing the rich to help the poor.

Just as the Democrats, who were generally liberal, had a conservative pro-slavery faction in the South, so too did the Whigs, who were generally conservative, have a liberal anti-slavery faction in the North. Northern Whigs regarded the enslavement of human beings as shameful, and demanded that it be abolished throughout the country, while southern Whigs tended to agree with southern Democrats that slavery should be allowed to continue. Eventually this disagreement broke the Whigs apart. In the 1850s, most of the pro-slavery southern Whigs joined the Democrats. The idealistic anti-slavery Whigs helped to found a new party: the Republicans.

The Republicans held their first convention in 1856. At that time they believed that slavery could be permitted to remain in those states where it was still legal, but that it must be prohibited in any new state that entered the Union. Later they demanded that slavery be abolished everywhere. Other than that, the Republicans followed the Whig policies in many ways. They were the party of Big Business, and called for a dynamic expansion of the nation's economy. The Republicans supported government aid to railroads, a strong banking system, and a sound monetary system. They were more interested in the needs and problems of the industrialized North than they were in those of the rural South and West. Only a few years after they were founded, the Republicans succeeded in electing a President: Abraham Lincoln. His election, though, split the nation apart on the slavery issue.

After the Civil War, the Republicans ruled the United States in an almost dictatorial way. The South was forced to submit to Reconstruction and was crushed under the carpetbagging Republicans from the North. Those who had been on the winning side in the war regarded it as their patriotic duty to vote Republican and keep the South in check. It was a bad time to be a Democrat, either in the North or in the South. Northern Democrats had generally supported the Civil War, but their loyalty to the Union won them few rewards from the dominant Republicans. Southern Democrats were powerless against the carpetbaggers, who had the aid of Federal troops and the votes of 700,000 recently freed slaves.

The Republicans now were the party of northern businessmen. They forgot most of the ideals that they had believed in when they were founded, and dedicated themselves to the pleasant pastime of getting rich. Since they did not favor a strong central government, Federal land and other property, including valuable timber and mining resources, were sold to private interests. The government officials in charge of these sales took huge bribes, and then sold the property at low prices to those who bribed them. The nation was the victim; the businessmen and their friends in high office were the gainers.

This was the period when great fortunes were being made by such men as John D. Rockefeller, Jay Gould, Cornelius Vanderbilt, and J. P. Morgan—tycoons of oil, railroads, and banking. These men operated as they pleased, with government blessing. "Law? What do I care about law?" cried Vanderbilt. "Hain't I got the power?" Bribery of legislatures, manipulation of stock markets, secret deals among the multi-millionaires to squeeze out competitors—all this was standard procedure in this era of rough, raw business practice. President Grant made no move to interfere. He regarded the tycoons as his friends, and let them do as they pleased. The naïve, simple Grant greatly enjoyed being President, and happily accepted expensive presents from his millionaire friends without seeing anything wrong with it. His friends stole millions from the government, celebrating their thefts over champagne and cigars at the White House, while Grant beamed in delight.

A day of reckoning had to come for the carefree Republicans of the Grant era. They had looted and drained the defeated South, they had run the country as their own private property, they had shrugged off the angry outcries of farmers and workingmen, they had even survived the Liberal Republican reform movement of 1872. But the Panic of 1873, ushering in unemployment, hunger, and misery, awakened the voters from their long sleep. The bloody uprisings against the carpetbaggers in the South caused more trouble. Most fair-minded Northerners were coming to believe that it was time to get the troops out of the southern states and let them rule themselves. The Republicans suddenly were very shaky on their throne. The elections of 1874 nearly pushed them off entirely. It was clear now that the South would stay Republican only by force of Federal arms; and the North, too, was weary of Republican rule.

One of the big issues of the day was "cheap money," an outgrowth of the Panic of 1873. During the war and in the prosperous years just after it, farmers in the West had borrowed heavily from eastern bankers to finance their own expansion. Wheat was selling at high prices, so the farmers took big loans to pay for new farm equipment and more land. Then came the Panic. The prices of commodities fell, because people were out of work and could not afford to purchase much. Wheat, which had been selling for $1.25 a bushel, dropped to about 60¢ a bushel. But the farmer's costs remained as high as ever. He had to pay the interest on his loans and mortgages—at a rate set when wheat was going at a high price. He had to pay shipping charges to get his grain to eastern markets—and the railroad tycoons kept the railroad tolls high. He had to repay some of the money he had borrowed—at a time when his earning power was low. To the farmer, a drop in the price of wheat was the same thing as a rise in the value of the dollar. In 1867, he could exchange a hundred bushels of wheat for $125. Now he could get only $60 for the same amount of wheat.

"Cheap money" was the answer. The farmers and others who were hard hit in 1873 demanded that the government print a lot of paper money and put it into circulation. The money then in use was backed by gold. Most people used gold coins, like the big double eagle, which was worth $20. The paper money of the time could be exchanged at any bank for gold coins; and since the value of gold was high, such paper money never lost its value.

The farmers wanted "greenbacks"—money backed by the credit of the government, but not redeemable in gold. Such money would not be as satisfying as a thick, shining double eagle—and so its value would drop in relation to the price of goods. It would take more of these new paper dollars to buy a hundred bushels of wheat than it had taken in the days of gold-backed currency. The farmers would have more dollars that they could use to pay off their loans to the eastern bankers.

Of course, the bankers were against this. If a farmer had borrowed a thousand dollars in gold, he ought to pay back a thousand dollars in gold—not in worthless greenbacks. The bankers were mostly Republicans. They influenced President Grant to resist the cry for cheap money. However, some Republicans from the farming states of the West took the opposite view. They knew that their own political futures depended on keeping the voters in their states happy—and the voters wanted greenbacks. So one Republican faction, led by Senator Oliver Morton of Indiana, supported the cheap money movement. Meanwhile the Democrats were just as divided. Southern Democrats, who were mainly agriculturalists and plantation owners, liked the idea of restoring prosperity by printing new money. In the Midwest, there still were many Democrats of the Andrew Jackson variety, who hated the eastern money interests and backed measures that would ease the lot of the ordinary citizen. They, too, wanted greenbacks. But in New York there were influential Democrats who were as wealthy as any of the Republican bankers. They opposed the Republicans on the issue of graft, but supported them on financial measures. These "hard money" Democrats included some of the most powerful men in the party; and they spoke out against greenbacks.

The problem was complex, and the politicians were split and uncertain over how to deal with it. It seemed clear that most of the people wanted cheap money. In the spring of 1874, the Republican-dominated Congress passed a law permitting the printing of a small supply of greenbacks. But even this halfway measure was too much for that most Republican of Presidents, Ulysses S. Grant. He vetoed it at the insistence of the business interests, and Congress did not dare to override the veto. This was one of the things that hurt the Republicans in that fall's election. The people spoke—and the anti-greenback Congressmen were swept from office in state after state.

The outgoing representatives still had a chance to pass laws. In those days the newly elected Congress did not meet until March, and Congressmen defeated the previous November held their seats for the intervening four months. These defeated members were known as "lame ducks." A Congress full of lame ducks came back to Washington early in 1875, determined to settle the money question before the Democratic Congressmen took office. Under the leadership of Senator John Sherman of Ohio, they worked out a bill that was so complicated that no one could say if it favored the farmers or the bankers. It improved the monetary system of the nation, thereby helping the plight of the small people, but at the same time it put more financial power into the hands of the tycoons. The Republicans thus could tell the great mass of voters that their wishes had been granted—while also keeping the bankers and manufacturers happy.

On March 4, 1875, the new Congress was sworn in at last. The Senate was still Republican, but the House looked strangely different. Most of the Radical Republicans of the 1860s were gone, some because they had died or retired, others because they had been defeated. Some of these men had hated the white South to the point of madness, but many of them had been idealistic and honest, favoring social reform. A lot of the Stalwart Republicans were gone, too; these were the grafters and bribe-takers, mostly, who had no strong feelings about the South but who looked after the interests of Big Business. In their place were Democrats from the South, eager to undo the effects of Reconstruction, and Democrats from the North, just as eager to clean up Republican corruption. To these newly elected southern Democrats, the presence of seven Negroes in the House of Representatives and one in the Senate seemed a symbol of Reconstruction that infuriated them. To the newly elected northern Democrats, the work at hand was an exposure of the evils of "Grantism."

Congress met for only about three weeks that March, and spent all its time discussing the problems of Louisiana, where another disputed election had been held and the carpetbaggers and the Democrats were at each other's throats. Another compromise was arranged, and then, on March 24, Congress adjourned. There was so little business for it to transact that it would not meet again until December.

There was trouble in the South during the summer months. Four states were still under carpetbagger rule—Mississippi, Louisiana, South Carolina, and Florida. The white Democrats, encouraged by their victories elsewhere, set out now to redeem these four.

Mississippi, which was due to have a state election in 1875, was the first to seek redemption. The Democrats there were determined to regain control, peacefully if possible, by force if necessary. One Mississippi newspaper openly declared, "All other means having been exhausted to abate the horrible condition of things, the thieves and robbers, and scoundrels, white and black, deserve death and ought to be killed. . . . [The carpetbaggers] ought to be compelled to leave the state or abide the consequences." The Democrats formed a private military force, armed with rifles, and drilled and marched, parading through Negro areas to terrify the voters. Negroes were forced at rifle point to listen to Democratic political speeches. Republican rallies were broken up by mobs of armed white men. Democrats brandishing guns stood in front of county courthouses to keep Negroes from registering to vote.

The Republican Governor of Mississippi, General Adelbert Ames, asked the Federal government for help. But Grant knew that sending government troops to the South was becoming unpopular in the North. Ohio was also having a state election in 1875, and a delegation of Ohio Republicans told the President that if he interfered in Mississippi, the Republicans would lose Ohio. Grant took heed of the warning. A member of his cabinet told Governor Ames that the country was "tired of these annual autumnal outbreaks in the South," and left Ames to shift for himself. The policy of sustaining Republican rule in the South by armed might had become so tarnished that Grant was abandoning it.

In September 1875 race riots broke out in Mississippi. White riflemen killed a number of Negroes. Governor Ames ordered the rifle companies to disband. The whites ignored his order. Ames considered forming a state militia, since he could not get Federal troops to keep the peace. But no white man in Mississippi, except a few scalawags, would join such a militia; Ames saw that it would be made up entirely of Negroes, which would lead to a war of black against white in the state. At that point he gave up and realized that nothing could save Mississippi for the Republicans.

On Election Day, thousands of thoroughly frightened Negroes hid in their cabins or fled to the safety of the swamps. Those who tried to vote were driven away from the polls by gunfire. The only Negroes permitted to cast ballots were those who had agreed in advance to vote for the Democrats. In three Mississippi counties, the Republicans got a total of 23 votes. The election was a clean sweep for the Democrats. The new legislature promptly impeached all Negro officeholders, forced the resignation of Governor Ames, and otherwise finished the job of redeeming Mississippi.

A month after the Mississippi election, Congress returned to Washington, opening its session on December 6, 1875. Choosing of officers was the first order of business. The important post of Speaker of the House went to Michael C. Kerr, a Democratic Representative from Indiana. Thomas W. Ferry, a Michigan Republican, was elected President of the Senate. Usually, the presiding officer of the Senate is the Vice-President of the United States; but Vice-President Henry Wilson had died on November 22, 1875. Since a new Vice-President would not take office until March 1877, the Senate had to choose one of its own members to wield the gavel at its meetings. This would prove to be an important matter when the controversy over the 1876 election began.

The Democrats now set about the task of investigating Republican corruption.

Actually, the Republicans had begun the job of exposing graft themselves. In the summer of 1874, Grant had chosen as his Secretary of the Treasury a former Civil War general, Benjamin H. Bristow of Kentucky. Bristow was no Stalwart and no friend of grafters. He came into the government sternly determined to clean things up, even if it hurt his own party. As he studied the records of the Treasury Department, Bristow observed that the amounts collected for Federal liquor taxes were strangely low. During 1873 and 1874 alone, some $4,000,000 in tax money had failed to reach the Treasury. Quietly Bristow sent special investigators to the various revenue offices. His work was thwarted by President Grant's own private secretary, Orville Babcock. Just as Bristow's detectives were about to visit the St. Louis revenue office, Babcock sent word to the conspirators there, who hastily fixed their records to make them look proper. When he realized that Babcock was working against him, Bristow organized a lightning raid, planning everything in code, and struck before the grafters had time to conceal the evidence of their crimes. On May 10, 1875, Bristow's inspectors burst into the revenue offices and rounded up the evidence. Some 350 members of the "Whiskey Ring" in St. Louis, Milwaukee, and Chicago were arrested. They had been siphoning the income from the liquor tax into their own bank accounts.

"Let no guilty man escape," President Grant told Bristow. The members of the Whiskey Ring went on trial and eventually went to prison. But when Bristow expressed an interest in investigating other officials, Grant decided that the reformer was too dangerous, and forced him to resign.

Grant could silence the troublesome Bristow that way, but he could not silence the Democrats in Congress. The early months of 1876 were nightmarish for the Republicans as scandal after scandal came to light. In February, Grant's ambassador to Great Britain, a prominent Ohio Republican, was forced to resign and leave England; he had been selling worthless mining stock to British investors. A month later, it was discovered that Secretary of War William W. Belknap had grown wealthy over the past six years by taking bribes from the operators of Indian trading posts at Army forts in the West. Grant allowed Belknap to resign before he could be impeached. Next came exposure of corruption in the Navy, Interior, and Post Office departments. "The President was overwhelmed," said one leading Republican newspaperman. "Wherever he turned some new dishonor lay concealed." None of the scandals involved Grant personally; but the revelations of early 1876 showed that the easygoing President had been shockingly unaware of what had been going on in his Administration.

And 1876 was a presidential election year.

Grant had been thinking, for a while, about running for re-election. His attitude was that the presidency was such great fun that it was a pity to give it up. For most of his life he had been unimportant, a nobody; during the war he had been a general, but he had had to endure uncomfortable battlefield conditions. Now, as President, he was comfortable at last. He lived in a great mansion, the White House. He earned a high salary. He received costly gifts from his businessmen friends; and leading men of Wall Street saw to it that the President made money in the stock market. He smoked the finest cigars; his wife enjoyed the best perfumes, the costliest jewelry. Whenever he went outdoors, cheering throngs hailed him with enthusiasm. There was scarcely any work involved in being President, and he had advisers to handle all the hard thinking for him, anyway. Why part with such a pleasant experience? Why not run for a third term?

The trouble was that no President in the history of the United States had ever served three terms. Only a few had served even twice: Washington, Jefferson, Madison, Monroe, Jackson, and Lincoln. Many Americans believed that the President should stay in office only four years; more than that was considered undemocratic. Lincoln had been the only two-term President since 1837, except for Grant, and Lincoln had been elected the second time in wartime, when it was dangerous to change leaders. When

Grant began thinking about a *third* term, even his own friends were shocked.

In December of 1875 the House of Representatives passed a resolution aimed directly at Grant's ambitions, declaring that a third term for any President would be "unwise, unpatriotic, and fraught with peril to our free institutions." The vote was 234 to 18; Republicans and Democrats alike joined forces to block Grant. The President took the hint and agreed that he would retire from office when his term ended on March 4, 1877. That left the field open for ambitious men of both parties. As 1876 began, the chief question in the land was, Who will run for President?

The Republicans, though badly hurt by the scandals of Grant-ism, still had hopes of victory in the election. They had won three presidential elections in a row; why not a fourth? The financial panic was ending. They expected that the normally Republican northern states, which had gone Democratic under the unusual conditions of 1874, would come back to the fold. True, they had lost control of much of the South in the past few years. But carpetbag Republicans still ruled three southern states. Though the others would probably go Democratic, that in itself could be used to frighten the North into backing the Republicans. The bloody shirt would be waved again in 1876.

Grant was eliminated, but the Republicans had no shortage of other would-be candidates. The best known of these was James G. Blaine of Maine, the most popular Republican in the country. Blaine was then forty-six years old, perhaps a little young for the Presidency, but no one could question his political experience. From 1869 to 1874 he had been Speaker of the House of Representatives. After the Republican defeat of that year, he had lost that post, but was still the leader of the Republicans in Congress. He was a large, commanding-looking man, a brilliant orator with a marvelous theatrical ability to excite and arouse his listeners, and an energetic, hard-working legislator. A vivid, colorful, attractive figure, Blaine seemed to many to be destined for the White House.

He had a special political advantage: despite his prominence, he had avoided involvement with any of the extremist Republican factions. More moderate than the Radicals, he did not have to bear the blame for the evils of Reconstruction in the South. More honest than the Stalwarts, he had never been implicated in the corruptions of Grantism, and was free from the stain of scandal that darkened the reputations of so many other Republicans. Blaine was the leader of a middle-of-the-road faction of Republicans nicknamed the Half-Breeds. They did not defend the corruption of the Grant Administration, but they did not attack it either; they were not vindictive toward the South, but they made no move to ease the injustices of Reconstruction. But these were disadvantages too, in some ways. Because he had not fought in the Civil War and had not been a vigorous Radical after it was over, Blaine could be accused of being "soft on slavery," which could hurt him in the North. And because he had looked with disdain on the misdeeds of the Stalwarts, he had many foes among the leadership of his party.

The most bitter enemy Blaine had was an arch-Stalwart, Senator Roscoe Conkling of New York, who also had presidential ambitions. A tall, muscular man with curly red hair and an elegant beard, Conkling prided himself on his good looks, and preened himself vainly before his mirror. He was the Republican boss of New York State, and took full advantage of his power, using his considerable influence on behalf of business interests and making himself and his friends wealthy. Conkling, unlike Blaine, belonged to Grant's inner circle of cronies. The scandals uncovered in 1876 left Conkling under suspicion, and he realized that he had no chance of being elected President, since the voters rightly regarded him as one of the most corrupt men in public life. Yet he was determined to do everything in his power to hurt Blaine's chances to get the nomination. Conkling had hated Blaine since 1866, when the two men had clashed in a debate in the House of Representatives. Conkling had made some slighting remarks about Blaine, who retaliated by unleashing a devastating volley of sarcasm. Blaine spoke of Conkling's "haughty disdain, his grandiloquent swell, his majestic, super-eminent, overpowering turkey-gobbler strut," and Conkling, wounded in his vanity, never forgave him.

A third contender was Senator Oliver P. Morton of Indiana, the last of the Radical Republicans. Morton, filled with hatred for the white South, could count on the votes of the carpetbaggers and scalawags there, and his cheap money ideas won backing for him in the farming states of the Middle West. But Morton had no followers in the all-important Northeast, where Republican strength was greatest. He was feared there as a narrow-minded, vengeful man whose monetary policies were unsatisfactory to the bankers and whose racial views were so extreme that they could lead to a new Civil War if he were elected. Morton, too, was a member of Grant's faction of the party, which opened him to charges of corruption. Worst of all, his health was poor; though he was only fifty-two, he suffered from a paralysis that forced him to use crutches at all times, and it was doubtful that he could survive the strain of the presidency. Nevertheless, Morton's political connections gave him a leading place in the struggle for the nomination.

There were a number of minor hopefuls, but no one took any of them very seriously. Benjamin Bristow, the deposed Secretary of the Treasury, was the favorite of the reform-minded Republicans; he was too much of a threat to the Stalwarts, though, to get nominated. John F. Hartranft, Governor of Pennsylvania, was occasionally mentioned as a possible candidate, as was the former Postmaster General, Marshall Jewell. The Governor of Ohio, Rutherford B. Hayes, was mentioned as a compromise candidate if the struggle among Blaine, Conkling, and Morton should knock all three out of the running. Hayes was not well known outside his own state, but he was a proven vote-getter there, and had shown himself to be a capable administrator. His best qualification for the nomination was a negative one: he had no enemies in the Republican Party.

The Democrats were also confident of victory in 1876. They felt that Grant had led the Republicans to the brink of ruin, and that the nation believed the time had come to "turn the rascals out." The Republicans could be blamed for corruption, financial panics, and the military suppression of the South. The Democrats could offer themselves as the party of integrity, a sound economy, and national harmony. They drew their support from many groups: the plantation aristocracy of the South, the cheap-money farmers of the Middle West, the rich merchants of the eastern seaboard, and the poor workers of the big cities who had recently come to this country from Ireland, Germany, and other European lands. Even the Republicans expected the Democrats to win the election. Rutherford B. Hayes noted in his diary on October 12, 1875, *"Defeat in the next Presidential election is almost a certainty."* He did not then suspect that he would be the Republican candidate in that election.

There was little doubt who the Democratic candidate would be. As 1876 opened, Governor Samuel J. Tilden of New York was far in the lead. This sixty-two-year-old bachelor, whose health was weak and whose personality was chilly, hardly seemed like a politician at all. He had become rich as a corporation lawyer; he collected rare books and fine wines; to the man in the street he was a remote, aristocratic figure. But Tilden had long been deeply involved in Democratic politics in New York State. Forty years before, when hardly out of his boyhood, he had been a valued adviser to President Martin Van Buren. As he rose to success in the business world, Tilden came to dominate the New York Democrats, though he preferred for a long time to work behind the scenes and let other men run for public office. He was cold and calculating, a man who never married because, as one of his friends explained, "He never felt the need of a wife. . . . Women were, so far as he could see, unimportant to his success." But Tilden always maintained unswerving honesty in his business and political dealings. In an era marked by private and public corruption, he stood out as a man of extraordinary virtue. When New York City fell into the hands of a sinister ring of crooked politicians, Tilden led the crusade against the thieves and drove them from office. A few years later, in 1874, he ran for Governor of New York and was elected, smashing Roscoe Conkling's corrupt political machine. Tilden won national fame the following year by uprooting another ring of grafters who had been looting the government of New York State. Now, Americans everywhere seemed to be begging him to carry his cleanup campaign to a third and even greater arena—the national government itself.

Tilden was not without opponents for the Democratic nomination. The cheap-money forces were behind Senator Thomas A. Hendricks of Indiana, because Tilden, as a rich Easterner, was known to dislike the idea of printing greenbacks. Hendricks was Tilden's only strong rival, though other candidates were in the field, such as the war hero Winfield Scott Hancock, and former Governor Joel Parker of New Jersey. Practical politicians disregarded these figures, and Hendricks as well. Tilden was the man for '76. The leaders of the Republican Party had only one main topic of discussion in the early months of 1876: finding a man who was strong enough to beat Tilden.

The more they thought about it, the less likely it seemed that any Republican could turn the trick. The White House seemed destined to slip into the hands of the Democrats. The way matters stood in the spring of 1876, only a miracle could keep Samuel J. Tilden from becoming President of the United States.

3

————————»«()»«————————

Choosing the Candidates

No Republican wanted the chance to run against Tilden more eagerly than James G. Blaine—and probably no Republican of the day was better qualified to be President. But Blaine knew he had many obstacles to overcome before he could get the nomination. He had to triumph over the enmity of Conkling and the other Stalwarts; he had to gain the favor of Grant, who was cool toward him; and he had to show that he hated the South. That last part was most important, for any Republican candidate had to appeal to the sympathies of a vast group of northern Civil War veterans.

Blaine had never waved the bloody shirt before, but now he set out to do it with a vengeance. In January 1876 Congress was debating a bill that would forgive those Confederate officials who were still banned from public office. Blaine, who had always taken a mild approach to the defeated South, was expected to support the bill. Instead he came forward on January 10 and delivered a thundering attack on Jefferson Davis, the President of the Confederacy. Blaine demanded that Davis be excluded from the amnesty bill, and accused the southern leader of personal guilt in the death of northern prisoners of war at the notorious Andersonville prison camp. Summoning up all his theatrical abilities, Blaine cried, "Some of us had kinsmen there, most of us had friends there, all of us had countrymen there, and in the name of these kinsmen, friends, and countrymen, I here protest . . . against calling back and crowning with the honors of full American citi-

zenship the man that organized that murder." Dramatically, his
voice throbbing with patriotic fervor, he solemnly declared "before
God, measuring my words, knowing their full extent and import,"
that none of the massacres in history, not even "the thumbscrews
and engines of torture of the Spanish Inquisition, begin to compare in atrocity with the hideous crime of Andersonville."

Blaine's speech was a cheap, deplorable political stunt. He did
not mean a word of it, regarding it merely as "sound strategy"
designed to whip up fear of the rebels. He simply hoped to in-
flame the public with the old emotions of the bitter war, for his
own advantage. The war veterans cheered Blaine wildly, while
the Democrats, who had regarded him as a force for national
harmony and even as a friend, were stunned. In the past, Blaine
had tried to be a statesman; now he descended to the lowest
depths of politics.

In the short run Blaine's cynicism paid off. He won the applause of South-haters in many states, and that winter his name
was frequently mentioned for the presidency. In state after state,
Republican leaders came out in favor of Blaine. But his sudden
triumph stiffened the determination of his enemies to cut him
down. Word leaked out that Blaine was guilty of taking bribes
from the Union Pacific Railroad. Specifically, he was accused of
having "sold" the Union Pacific a batch of worthless bonds for
$64,000, and then to have helped the Union Pacific get favorable
treatment in Congress.

Blaine tried to deny the charges. He went before Congress in
April to defend himself, claiming that his dealings with the railroad had been a simple business transaction. Considering the sort
of chicanery most Congressmen then indulged in, Blaine was
right; by the standards of the time Blaine was innocent. Nevertheless, now he was tinged with corruption in the eyes of the public,
and it hurt him badly. The liberal reform wing of the Republicans,

already disturbed over Blaine's inflammatory speech of January 10, came to regard him as wholly unacceptable because of the Union Pacific scandal. The liberals increasingly turned to Benjamin Bristow, the conqueror of the Whiskey Ring, as their man.

Still, Blaine remained the front runner for the nomination as the time neared for the choosing of candidates. His spirited self-defense won back support in May. As the attack on him continued, he appeared before packed galleries in the House of Representatives on June 5, carrying a package of letters he had written to the stockbroker who had handled his Union Pacific transaction. All spring he had been urged to make these letters public. Drawing them from his pocket, he slammed them down on his desk and shouted, "There they are!" The audience gasped in surprise. Then, timing his words for maximum effect, Blaine declared, "I invite the confidence of 44,000,000 of my countrymen while I read those letters from this desk." When he read them, adding his own commentary, it appeared as though he were wholly blameless. Only later was it discovered that he had not read the letters in their proper order, had skipped incriminating passages in some, and had omitted several letters entirely.

It seemed as if Blaine had regained the commanding position he had held in the winter. The Republican convention was due to meet in Cincinnati on June 14, 1876, and it looked certain that Blaine would be nominated despite everything. But on June 11—a hot, muggy day in Washington—Blaine collapsed on the steps of his church after having walked a mile from his home. He was unconscious for two days—a victim of fatigue and strain. Word went out that he was dying. On Tuesday, the day before the opening of the convention, Blaine recovered, and telegraphed the delegates in Cincinnati that he would soon be on his feet. The collapse hurt his cause, though, for it raised the question of his physical fitness for the presidency.

Republican leaders from all over the nation were flocking to Cincinnati in a mood of high excitement. Not since Lincoln's nomination in 1860 had there been a real contest for the nomination; in 1864 Lincoln's renomination had been inevitable, and Grant had been an easy winner in 1868 and 1872. This year there was going to be a fight. Would Blaine get the bid? Or would his many enemies find some way to stop him at the last moment?

Everyone knew that the two best-known rivals—Conkling and Morton—were unable to get the nomination for themselves. Conkling was too deeply stained by corruption, and Morton was too bitter an enemy of the South, as well as being in poor health. Bristow, the reformer, could never hope to win the backing of the Stalwarts. If Blaine were to be stopped, the convention would have to turn to a dark horse—one of the lesser-known men. But which one?

The name of Rutherford B. Hayes was now being mentioned quite often as the only one who might be able to take the nomination away from Blaine. Nobody—least of all Hayes—would have believed, a year earlier, that such a thing was possible. Now, suddenly, Hayes had emerged as a strong candidate.

Hayes was an important figure in Ohio, but not well known outside that state. He had been elected to Congress in 1864 and again in 1866, but in his three years in Washington he never made a speech or offered an opinion on the great issues of the day. In 1867 he was elected Governor of Ohio, and he was re-elected in 1869. After retiring from public office for a few years to practice law, he was elected to the governorship again in 1875. He was a pleasant, rather serious-minded man, modest and cautious, who had never said anything to offend anyone and so had no enemies. Among his Ohio friends were some shrewd politicians who thought they could push him into the White House. Hayes was willing though not eager to become President; it flattered him to think that he was considered worthy of the job, but he had his own private doubts. He had noted in his diary on April 14, 1875:

I am still importuned in all quarters to consent to run as Republican candidate for Governor. Several suggest that if elected Governor now, I will stand well for the Presidency next year. How wild! What a queer lot we are becoming! Nobody is out of the reach of that mania.

The man behind Hayes' candidacy was Senator John Sherman of Ohio, a cunning, highly intelligent man with a justified reputation as a financial wizard. Sherman was too cold a personality to run for President himself; in many ways he was similar to Tilden, whom he admired and respected greatly. If he could not be a President, perhaps he could make a President. In 1875, once he realized he could not have the nomination himself, Sherman began to tempt Hayes with dreams of the White House, and found Hayes interested.

Sherman got Hayes' campaign going on January 21, 1876, by releasing to the public an open letter to his fellow Ohioan, State Senator A. M. Burns. Sherman declared, "The election of a Democratic President means a restoration to full power in the government of the worst elements of the rebel Confederacy. . . . If it [the South] should elect a President and both Houses of Congress, the constitutional amendments would be disregarded, the freedmen would be nominally citizens but really slaves . . . the power of the general government would be crippled, and the honors won by our people in subduing rebellion would be a subject of reproach rather than of pride. The only safeguard from these evils is the election of a Republican President, and the adoption of a liberal Republican policy which should be fair and even generous to the South, but firm in the maintenance of all the rights won by the war."

Having struck the proper tone of northern righteousness, Sherman went on to say, "Among the candidates now generally named, I have no such preference that I could not heartily support either of them [Blaine or Bristow]. They are men of marked ability, who have rendered important public services, but, considering all things, I believe the nomination of Governor Hayes would give us the more strength, taking the whole country at large, than any other man. He is better known in Ohio than elsewhere, and is stronger there than elsewhere, but the qualities that have made him strong in Ohio will . . . make him stronger in every state."

Sherman's recital of Hayes' qualifications was something less than exciting: "He was a good soldier, and, though not greatly distinguished as such, he performed his full duty, and I noticed . . . that the soldiers who served under him loved and respected him. As a Member of Congress he was not a leading debater, or manager in party tactics, but he was always sensible, industrious, and true to his convictions and the principles and tendencies of his party, and commanded the sincere respect of his colleagues. As a governor, thrice elected, he has shown good executive abilities and gained great popularity. . . . He is fortunately free from the personal enmities and antagonisms that would weaken some of his competitors, and he is unblemished in name, character, or conduct. . . ."

There was nothing in the record of the "sensible, industrious" Hayes to compare with the public achievements of the famous Blaine. Blaine, because of his prominence, had made enemies and had made mistakes. Hayes had not. In the end, that made all the difference.

Hayes became the favorite of the anti-Blaine forces. Each of Blaine's rivals decided to support Hayes if he himself could not get the nomination. As the delegates arrived in Cincinnati, General Edward F. Noyes, chairman of the Ohio delegation, moved among them, striking deals on Hayes' behalf. Noyes approached the followers of Conkling, Morton, and Bristow, and urged them to back Hayes once it became clear that their own man could not win. The Blaine faction grew so worried by this that Blaine's manager tried to end the Hayes threat by offering him the Vice-Presidential spot on the Blaine-Hayes ticket. But the Hayes men would not accept the offer.

The convention opened on Wednesday morning, June 14. It met in a hall which, according to the New York *Tribune,* "covered over four acres, its architecture that of an ambitious and disappointed railroad depot, its decorations those of a country barbecue on a four-acre scale . . . and its roof an unsightly mass of beams and rafters." General Noyes delivered a welcoming speech on behalf of the host state, Ohio; he subtly attacked Blaine and praised Hayes without mentioning any names. "Give us a man of great purity of private life and an unexceptionable public record," Noyes urged.

The first important business was the adoption of the platform—a set of programs and principles which, in theory, the Republican Party claimed to support that year. The platform pointed with pride to the past, reminding the country who had won the Civil War, but also promised reform in the future. The Republicans demanded "honesty, fidelity, and capacity" in all appointments to public office. They pledged themselves to uphold the rights of all southern citizens, white and black, but avoided discussing the controversial policy of keeping Federal troops in the carpetbagger-ruled states. The touchy matter of cheap money also was mentioned only in the vaguest terms. The Democrats were bluntly denounced: the Republican platform all but threatened civil war if the Democrats won the election, declaring that a Democratic victory "would reopen sectional strife and imperil national honor and human rights."

On the second day came the nominating speeches. Marshall

Jewell of Connecticut was nominated first, to no one's great interest. Then Oliver Morton was placed in nomination with a speech that foolishly called attention to his ailments and disabilities. Bristow was nominated next, by John Harlan of Kentucky, who tactlessly enraged the Stalwarts by saying, "His mode has been to execute the law; and if the Republican Party contained offenders who betrayed their trust, or who were thieves, he let them be punished as well as anybody else." That seemed like a warning to the party leaders that Bristow might well be prosecuting them next.

A stir of excitement began as Colonel Robert G. Ingersoll of Illinois came forward to nominate Blaine. Ingersoll spoke for only five minutes, but it was a powerful oration that brought roars of enthusiasm from the delegates. Schoolboys for decades afterward would memorize and recite Ingersoll's speech, in which he cried that the American people "call for the man who has torn from the throat of treason the tongue of slander—for the man who has snatched the mask of Democracy from the hideous face of the rebellion. . . . Like an armed warrior, like a plumed knight, James G. Blaine marched down the halls of the American Congress and threw his shining lance full and fair against the brazen forehead of the defamers of his country and maligners of his honor. . . ." By the time Ingersoll had finished, the convention had been roused to such frantic excitement that Blaine might have been nominated by a landslide vote, if a vote had been taken just then. But there were three more candidates to be placed in nomination, and the frenzy subsided. Blaine, who would thereafter be known as the "Plumed Knight," had to be patient.

Conkling, Hayes, and Governor Hartranft of Pennsylvania were nominated. By then it was late evening; but the Blaine men, realizing that the convention still tingled from Ingersoll's speech, called for a vote that was likely to mean victory. At that moment the gas lights in the hall went out, and darkness forced an adjournment. There were those who whispered that an anti-Blaine man had sabotaged the lighting system to delay the balloting.

That night there was hectic backstage politicking. A meeting took place among the managers of Bristow, Morton, and Hayes. The Morton man agreed to support Hayes after the first ballot unless Morton showed unexpected strength. The Bristow man made the same pledge, after being promised that Hayes, if elected, would give a seat on the Supreme Court to John Harlan, Bristow's main backer.

On Friday, June 16, the first ballot was taken. The roll was called, with 378 votes needed for the nomination. Blaine got 285, Morton 124, Bristow 113, Conkling 99, Hayes 61, Hartranft 58, and Jewell 11; three votes were cast for William Wheeler, a New York politician connected with Conkling's machine. Blaine was within a hundred votes of the nomination. Hayes, running fifth, had been only three votes ahead of the obscure Hartranft. That hardly looked promising for the man from Ohio—but the first ballot results meant very little. Now the maneuvering and skirmishing would begin.

The Hayes men worked quietly to unite all the anti-Blaine Republicans behind their candidate. The strategy did not make itself apparent right away. On the second ballot, Blaine gained 11 votes to 296, Bristow gained one vote, and Hayes gained three. Morton and Conkling lost ground; Jewell dropped out altogether. The third and fourth ballots showed little change; Blaine was still far ahead, Bristow was second, and Morton and Conkling lost a few more delegates to Hayes, who was now running sixth, behind Hartranft. But the fifth ballot produced some drama. Michigan, which had 22 votes, had been divided, 11 for Bristow, 6 for Blaine, and 5 for Hayes. Now the chairman of the Michigan delegation rose and said, "Michigan casts her twenty-two votes for

Rutherford B. Hayes of Ohio." It was the first solid move toward Hayes.

He picked up 14 other votes on that ballot, to stand third with 104. Blaine had 286, Bristow 114. Morton, Conkling, and Hartranft had 246 votes among them—enough to decide the contest. Who would get those votes? This was the point in the convention when individual delegates would begin to break away from their delegations and offer their votes to one of the leading candidates in the hopes of gaining future favors. On the sixth ballot, Blaine added 22 votes, mostly at the expense of Hartranft, for a total of 308. That was only 70 short of nomination. Hayes moved into second place, far behind with 113; Bristow was third with 111. If enough of the delegates who had been voting for Conkling, Morton, or Hartranft switched to Blaine on the next roll call, the contest would be over.

This was the last chance to stop Blaine. The leaders of the New York and Pennsylvania delegations conferred. Morton, Conkling, Bristow, and Hartranft would step aside in favor of Hayes, lest the hated Blaine get the nomination. The roster of states was called, and Indiana—Morton's state—switched its 25 votes to Hayes. Next came Kentucky—Bristow's state. John Harlan, already seeing himself a member of the Supreme Court, cast Kentucky's votes for Hayes. Conkling's men delivered 61 of New York's 70 votes for Hayes. And so it went, state after state getting aboard the Hayes bandwagon while the dismayed followers of Blaine watched the certain nomination slip away. In the final total, Hayes had 384 votes, Blaine 351; 21 stubborn reformers stuck with Bristow to the end.

Hayes was properly humble in the face of the high honor. He had thought all along that Blaine would win the nomination. Early on the morning of June 16, Hayes had confided to his diary his first words of optimism: *There has been a gradual change on the 14th and 15th, and now it seems something more than a possibility that he [Blaine] will fail. If he fails, my chance, as a compromise candidate, seems to be better than that of any other candidate. So now we are in suspense. I have kept cool and unconcerned to a degree that surprises me. . . . I feel that defeat will be a great relief—a setting free from bondage. The great responsibility overpowers me.* And now the suspense was over; now the "great responsibility" was his to bear.

The convention finished its work by picking a candidate for Vice-President. The party leaders decided to choose a man from New York, since Tilden, Hayes' probable opponent, was a New Yorker. The roster of New York politicians was examined. Someone suggested Chester Alan Arthur, one of Roscoe Conkling's lieutenants. But Arthur, who was Collector of Customs for the Port of New York, was known to earn $40,000 a year in bribes and tips from merchants and importers trying to avoid paying customs fees; he was hardly a good choice in a year when the voters were demanding reform. So the second place on the ticket went to William A. Wheeler, another New Yorker whose record was clean. "Who is Wheeler?" Hayes had asked only a short time before. Now they would be together on the national ballot.

"Who is Hayes?" the rest of the country might well ask. The answers were none too complimentary. Henry Adams of Boston, the descendant of two Presidents himself, wrote at this time that Hayes is "a third rate nonentity, whose only recommendation is that he is obnoxious to no one." The great newspaperman Joseph Pulitzer, whose reform-minded New York *World* had been for Bristow, also found little to praise in the candidate: "Hayes has never stolen. Good God, has it come to this?" But Blaine, generous in defeat, sent a telegram of support to Hayes, and promised to work hard to bring about his election four months hence.

* * *

There was no drama when the Democrats met to pick their candidates in St. Louis on June 27. Victory was in the air, and Tilden seemed to be destiny's choice.

Even his enemies respected him. John Sherman, Hayes' leading backer, called Tilden "a man of singular political sagacity, of great shrewdness. . . . I knew Mr. Tilden personally and very favorably, as we were members of a board of railroad directors which frequently met. . . . He had acquired great wealth as the attorney of corporations, and was undoubtedly a man of marked ability."

Tilden had been toying with the idea of running for the nation's highest office at least since 1868. He did not really like the rough, strenuous business of campaigning, though, and in that year he arranged for the nomination to go to his friend Horatio Seymour. But after Tilden had broken up the shameful machine of New York City's Boss Tweed in 1871, cries of "Tilden for President" were frequently heard in a nation weary of corruption in high places. The same cries were heard after he smashed the Conkling machine in New York State in 1874. The following year, an influential Massachusetts newspaper, the Springfield *Republican,* ran an editorial under the heading, "Governor Tilden and the Presidency," inviting him to run. Friends and strangers bombarded him with letters asking him to think about seeking the office. He lacked those qualities usually thought important in candidates—warm-heartedness, sociability, humor. But his personality was irrelevant; the nation needed a tough, honest, intelligent President after eight years of Grant's slovenly regime, and Tilden met those requirements superbly.

Tilden did not need much convincing. He believed that it was his duty to the country to run for the Presidency, and he believed he could win. His clear judgment, hard-headed efficiency, and absolute honesty would save the nation from the grafters and corruptionists who infested every department of the government. When he launched his drive for the nomination, he did it in the methodical, resourceful way that had marked his earlier political triumphs and his private business career.

He knew that to most people he had the reputation of being a cold fish, more of a machine than a man. To overcome this, he organized what would today be called a public relations campaign to change his "image." No one had ever done such a thing before in American politics; Tilden set up a Newspaper Popularity Bureau, with a staff of editors, writers, and artists, and put it to work manufacturing a warm, lovable Samuel J. Tilden. Tons of press releases went out to 1,200 newspapers all over the country. They told the story of Tilden's life: his humble birth, his rise to fame and fortune, his fight against crooked politicians. Human-interest stories and cartoons, lively and amusing, were published almost every day. Whenever a public figure made a favorable comment about Tilden, it was copied and sent out to the papers by the Popularity Bureau. Tilden even foreshadowed modern political polling by sending men to college campuses with instructions to learn what the college students thought about the political situation. The students were most interested in political reform, Tilden learned—and they thought Tilden was the right man to clean up the government.

By the time the Democratic convention opened nearly everyone knew that Tilden stood for sound administration, the eradication of graft, the reduction of unnecessary government spending, and lower taxes. Democratic politicians in many states were on record in support of his candidacy, although the greenback advocates from the farming states preferred Senator Thomas A. Hendricks of Indiana. There were also some anti-Tilden Democrats in Tilden's own state of New York, men who had been exposed as rogues during his cleanup program; but their influence was slight. The South was for Tilden, although not very enthusiastically, since he was a Northerner and had favored the Civil War. Southern Democrats figured that it was better to have a Democratic President, even a northern one, than another Republican, and, since Tilden looked likely to win, they backed him.

The convention came to order in St. Louis shortly after noon on June 27. A perspiring crowd of 5,000 was on hand as Henry Watterson of Kentucky, the convention's chairman, delivered the first speech. "We are called together," said Watterson, "to determine by our wisdom whether honest government, administered by honest men, shall be restored to the American people." He pointed to the Panic of 1873, with its hard times, closed factories, and hungry citizens. He spoke of Republican corruption and carpetbaggery. He called for a clean sweep of the government: "It is the issue, not the man, that should engage us."

The adoption of the platform followed. The Democrats called for an end to the waste of public property, reform in taxes, tariffs, and the civil service, and a reduction in the national budget. Each paragraph of the platform began with the phrase, "Reform is necessary." Trouble arose over the greenback problem. Tilden, who had been responsible for most of the planks in the platform, believed in a strong currency backed with gold, and the platform advocated that position. The western faction of greenbackers rose to amend the platform to call for an immediate issue of paper money. When the matter came to a vote, the "hard money" forces won, 550 to 219. It was an indication of the way the rest of the convention would go.

Nominations began on the second day. Senator Thomas F. Bayard of Delaware was nominated first, then Thomas Hendricks of Indiana and Joel Parker, the Governor of New Jersey. When New York was called, Francis Kernan, one of Tilden's allies, placed his name in nomination. Then John Kelly, the leader of the Tammany Hall group of New York City politicians, got the floor to denounce Tilden. Kelly, whose political power had been broken by Tilden, shouted that the convention should give the nomination to Senator Hendricks. Angry delegates howled Kelly down, and his words were unheard. When order was restored, several other candidates were proposed, including William Allen of Ohio and General Winfield Scott Hancock of Pennsylvania. Then the voting began.

The winner would need a two-thirds majority—492 votes. On the first ballot, eighteen states gave all their votes to Tilden, and eleven more gave him partial support. He received 404½ votes, Hendricks 140½, Hancock 75, Allen 54, Bayard 33, and Parker 18. Missouri cast 16 votes for James O. Brodhead, but before the totals were announced seven of these votes were switched to Tilden, giving him 411½. He was only 81 votes from the nomination, and on the second ballot the delegates rushed to change their vote. Tilden picked up 6 votes from Colorado, 10 from Georgia, 4 from Illinois, 2 each from Iowa and Kansas. He was still 25 short. The switching continued; Iowa gave him 4 more, Illinois 2, and Missouri 21 to put him over the top. The delegates were on their feet, shouting out questions, demanding to know the total count. When the confusion ended, Tilden had 508 votes, Hendricks 75, Hancock 60, Allen 54, and several others a few votes apiece. A delegate from Pennsylvania moved that Tilden's nomination be made unanimous, and the convention adjourned for the night.

Compromise was in order the next day when the candidate for Vice-President was chosen. Tilden was an Easterner, a financial conservative, and a pro–Civil War Democrat. To balance these views, the convention unanimously awarded second place on the ticket to Senator Hendricks—a Westerner, a greenback man, and an advocate of the theory, so popular in the South, that "this is a white man's Government, made by the white man for the white man." Afterward, John Kelly of Tammany Hall took the floor to tell the delegates that although he had done all in his power to defeat Tilden for the nomination, no one would work harder to bring about his election. On that harmonious note, the united Democrats closed their convention, seeing only victory ahead.

Tilden had not gone to the convention. Candidates for nomination traditionally stay away from the meeting; Tilden had remained in Albany, performing the duties of the Governor of New York. A telegram from St. Louis brought him the good news. That night a brass band serenaded Tilden at his Albany residence, and bonfires were lit to celebrate his nomination. Tilden spoke to a group of visitors at the Executive Mansion, telling them, "The nomination was not made by the leaders of the party. It was the people who made it. They want reform. They have wanted it a long while, and, in looking about, they became convinced that it is to be found here." Letters and telegrams of congratulation poured in. "God is in this move!" wrote one Democrat. "Thank the Lord that we have reason to hail yourself as the coming President," wrote another. A strange feeling of joy spread through the land. Samuel J. Tilden was going to rescue America from the grafters.

A few days after the close of the Democratic gathering, the nation's attention turned away from the Hayes-Tilden contest to observe an important anniversary. On July 4, 1876, the United States of America was one hundred years old.

It was a savage irony that the centennial had arrived in such a year. What had become of the ideals of 1776? Where was the proud philosophy of Washington and Jefferson and Madison now? The soul of the land had been stained with blood; one American had taken up arms against another; the country had

been held together only through force. The war had ended, but
the bitterness of North toward South and South toward North remained. And the government itself had fallen into the hands of
greedy, shameless men who pilfered the public treasury without
conscience. Shabby little President Grant, a feeble successor to
the men of 1776, had disgraced his office, not through personal
corruption but through ignorance and incompetence. The real
power in the country had passed into the possession of a small
group of monopolists who were making themselves fantastically
wealthy at the expense of everyone else. This was America in the
centennial year.

But the great day could not be ignored even in this time of
national embarrassment. On July 4, millions of Americans pic-
nicked, listened to patriotic speeches, and shattered the air with
the explosions of fireworks. At Philadelphia a vast throng pushed
into Fairmount Park, where the Centennial Exposition, America's
first world's fair, was being held. Grant himself, the tainted President, had opened the magnificent Exposition. All the wonders of
science and industry were on display there, including an amazing
new machine called the telephone. On opening day, Dom Pedro,
the Emperor of Brazil, stood beside the exhibit of Alexander Gra-
ham Bell and put the strange device to his ear. "My God, it
talks!" the startled Emperor cried.

The Centennial Exposition was a marvelous success. The
Fourth of July all over the country was the liveliest party anyone
had ever known. The anniversary passed, and things settled back
to normal again. As the hot summer months dragged along,
Americans began to think seriously about the problem of picking
a new President to guide the land into its second century. Hayes?
Tilden? Tilden? Hayes? Back and forth the names were tossed. It
was time for a change, yes, time to throw the Republicans out.
This Tilden was a good man. But Hayes was a good man too,

untouched by scandal. Was Tilden really to be trusted? A man without a family, a man who was so rich—what did he know about the problems of the average American? On the other hand, if Hayes got in, wouldn't that mean more corruption among the Republican officeholders? Could Hayes control Conkling and that bunch?

Hayes. . . .

Tilden. . . .

The country debated. The country weighed man against man, party against party, issue against issue. Two things became clear: that Hayes and Tilden both were worthy of the high office, and that the election was going to be a close one.

No one, though, realized just how close it was actually going to be.

4

━━━━━◈━━━━━

Hayes Against Tilden

The election of 1876 was not one in which the personalities of the candidates were particularly important to the outcome. Still, a man could not run for President without having every aspect of his life held up for close examination by the public. The voters got to know both Hayes and Tilden reasonably well that summer. They found Tilden more interesting, more unusual—but Hayes was more likable, more human.

Hayes was a handsome, broad-shouldered man of medium height, with dark, deeply set blue eyes and a long curling beard. His life story was one of hard work, well-deserved success, and public service, always an important combination for anyone with presidential hopes. Born in Delaware, Ohio, in 1822, he grew up in the town of Lower Sandusky, now called Fremont. His father had died a few months before he was born; he was raised by his mother and her younger brother, Sardis Birchard, the greatest influence in Hayes' life.

Ohio was then on America's western frontier, and young Hayes lived in a small, rugged community just past the pioneer stage. However, he missed one political advantage by not being born in a log cabin. He was born in a brick house—the first one in his town, in fact. He was a sickly boy, but life on the frontier was good for him; he toughened and became sturdy, and when he was fifteen he made the long journey eastward to New England to enroll in a fine private academy in Middletown, Connecticut.

After a year's absence he returned to his beloved Ohio and enrolled in Kenyon College, near his family home. When college was in recess, Hayes walked the forty miles home to be with his mother and uncle; he walked even in December, when he had to fight his way through drifting snow.

He was a good student but showed no special brilliance; he was restless, full of uncertain ambitions, and dreamed of a military career, or perhaps of going into politics. He gave his allegiance to the conservative Whig Party, and when the Whig candidate, William Henry Harrison, was elected in 1840, eighteen-year-old Hayes declared: "I never was more elated in my life . . . Glorious!" What made Harrison's victory all the sweeter was that he was a fellow Ohioan—the first ever to be President. Hayes would be the second.

When he had his degree from Kenyon, he went to Harvard to study law, and in the spring of 1845 he set up in business as a lawyer in Lower Sandusky. There was little for a lawyer to do in that town, and Hayes spent most of his time reading, talking politics, and dreaming of some more exciting life. The most exciting thing he did in those years was to visit a friend in Texas. It was an immense journey, involving travel by railroad, stagecoach, and Mississippi River steamer. It gave him his first view of the slave-owning South, and he was surprised to see how neat the villages of slaves were, and how happy they seemed to be. (He did not get a chance to experience the darker side of slave life: the whippings, the hunger, the separation of families.) He was charmed by the climate of the South, writing, "I see a garden filled with the richest shrubbery, roses blooming and birds singing as if it were the first of June instead of January." He was agreeably amazed that the Texans were civilized; he had expected to find brawling frontiersmen, and instead he found elegant, charming aristocrats. (Hayes did not have the opportunity of seeing the harsher side of southern white life, either.) His journey left him with warm feelings for the South and its people, although his conscience twinged him a bit when he reflected that the comforts of southern life depended in large measure upon the enslavement of human beings.

In 1849 Hayes moved to Cincinnati, looking for the wider range of clientele that the big city could offer a rising young lawyer. Several months passed before he earned his first fee; but soon he was busy and prospering, making influential friends, and well enough established to take the bold step of finding a wife. In 1852 he married Lucy Ware Webb, an attractive, intelligent Cincinnati girl of a good family. He borrowed four thousand dollars from Uncle Sardis and bought a house, and opened a larger law office.

Still, Hayes' place in the world was a modest one, and he knew it better than anyone. In January 1855, he wrote in his diary: *Two things are now ascertained. . . . One is, that I have neither health nor capacity to be a first-class figure in my profession; the other, that I appear to have enough of both to acquire a reasonable success—enough for happiness. With this I am content.*

He was thrifty, prudent, diligent; again and again he accused himself of "too much light reading" and told himself that he must "become more energetic by tough reading." He pored over works of history, biography, philosophy. He went skillfully and busily about the practice of law. He worried much about improving his mind, but abandoned his earlier romantic notions of becoming a great general, a statesman, a national leader. He was earnest, sober-minded, serious, and rather commonplace.

His only hobby was politics. When the Whigs collapsed in the 1850s, he joined the new Republican Party, attracted more by its conservative views on financial matters than by its strong anti-slavery stand. With his typically conservative opinions about the sanctity of private property, Hayes found it hard to insist that the slaveowners be forced to give up their slaves. But gradually the injustice of a situation whereby human beings could be anyone's private property dawned on him, and he began to oppose slavery more strongly. Still, he was never very passionate about it. "I must study the subject," he told his diary, "and am now beginning with Clarkson's *History of the Abolition of the Slave Trade.*" When Hayes condemned slavery, it was less out of personal belief than out of a wish to follow the policy of the Republican Party. First and last, Hayes was loyal to his party.

His party repaid him in 1858 by electing him to the post of City Solicitor of Cincinnati, at the handsome salary for that era of $3,500 a year. It was the first time he had run for office, and he won a close contest against a strong rival. He performed his duties capably, and found the job congenial; he was planning to run for re-election when the long nightmare of the Civil War began.

He had watched the approach of war in the late 1850s with deep uneasiness. Basically a reasonable, logical-minded man, he went on hoping that North and South could resolve their disagreements peacefully right up to the moment when the cannons began to boom. As the southern states pulled out of the Union one by one late in 1860 and early in 1861, Hayes was quite willing to let them go without a struggle. Twenty states were left, stretching from Atlantic to Pacific; that was still a glorious enough country, without the slaveowners! He had no wish to make war to compel the slave states to return to the fold. But when fighting began in the spring of 1861, his outlook changed. The Union itself was threatened; the free states had to be defended, the slave states punished for their defiance of the Constitution. "This is a holy war," he said, "and if a fair chance opens I shall go into it; if a fair chance don't open, I shall perhaps take measures to open one."

He was nearly forty years old and had never seen military action before. Yet this settled, prosperous, middle-aged lawyer felt he had to join the Army, whatever the risks. "I would prefer to go into it," he declared, "if I knew that I was to die or be killed in the course of it, than to live through and after it without taking any part in it." He resigned as City Solicitor and applied for the post of an officer in Ohio's 23rd Regiment. In June 1861 he received the rank of major and went off to war.

To some extent, Hayes was motivated by political necessity: he realized that anyone who hoped to win public office after the war would be asked to prove that he had served his country in battle. But it was also simple honorable patriotism that drew Hayes away from his home and onto the battlefield; he regarded it as any healthy man's obligation to volunteer to defend the Union. And there was that old yearning for excitement, now to be fulfilled.

Many of the politicians who became soldiers in 1861 cracked under the strain of war and swiftly were sent back to civilian life. Not Hayes. He found soldiering a tough, dangerous business, but he thrived on it. He discovered natural abilities for leading men under fire; he found hidden reserves of physical strength; he developed a boyish enthusiasm for the outdoor life. He went without sleep for thirty-six hours in a single stretch, and spent nineteen hours of one day in his saddle. Though not a brilliant officer, he was a brave one, and his ability to stay cool in moments of peril brought him several promotions. By the fall of 1861 he was a lieutenant colonel. He had been wounded several times, and the men whom he commanded regarded him as a valiant, inspiring leader. (One of his young soldiers was William McKinley, a future President.)

Back and forth across the war zone Hayes' regiment marched. He fought in West Virginia, Virginia, Maryland; in September 1862, he led a gallant charge up a hill occupied by Confederate gunners, and suffered a wound in his left arm. He lay beside a wounded Confederate on the field while the battle raged about them. "We were quite jolly and friendly," Hayes said later. "It was by no means an unpleasant experience." He was sent home for the winter to recover, but early in 1863 he was again at war in the West Virginia mountains, confident that the North would soon be victorious. As the struggle dragged on, he wearied of it; he felt it had become a barbarous conflict, and wished the South would finally admit defeat so the slaughter could end.

While fighting in Maryland in the summer of 1864, Hayes learned that his friends in Cincinnati were suggesting him as a candidate for Congress. The nomination was his for the asking, and he accepted it; but he wrote home to say that he would not come home to campaign for votes. "An officer fit for duty who at this crisis would abandon his post to electioneer for a seat in Congress ought to be scalped," Hayes wrote. "You may feel perfectly sure I shall do no such thing." He spent the month of September in the thick of the fighting, often baffled by the complexities of warfare, but never frightened. And on October 17, 1864, the voters of Cincinnati sent Hayes to Congress by a wide margin over his opponent.

When the new term of Congress began the following March, Hayes was still in uniform. He did not resign his commission and return to civilian life until June 1865. At the end of November he entered the House of Representatives. The war was over; Lincoln was dead; Andrew Johnson had begun his unhappy presidency, and the fierce Thaddeus Stevens was demanding vengeance against the South. During the stormy sessions of 1866, when President Johnson's power was broken and the Radical Republicans became supreme, the voice of Representative Hayes of Ohio was not heard in the halls of Congress. He quietly supported the Radicals in their program of Reconstruction, because he had fought for the Union and believed it was proper to impose strong terms upon the losers, but he stayed in the background. As always, he followed the leaders of his party. Hayes' own contribution to the work of Congress was to serve as chairman of the Library Committee. While the Radicals raged in fury against the rebels, Hayes droned on through committee meetings dealing with the purchase of books and the development of a botanical garden in Washington. By keeping silent on the burning issues of the day, Hayes avoided making enemies in the South or in the North, but it was hardly courageous of him.

In the 1866 elections he easily won a second term in Congress. Steadily, patiently, he gained reputation; the headlines went to such men as Thaddeus Stevens and James Blaine, but the quiet man from Ohio now was frequently seen at important meetings. While keeping out of controversy, he managed to impress the leading Republicans with his conscientiousness and industriousness. He impressed Ohio, too, and at the beginning of 1867 he was asked to run for Governor. Hayes was pleased by the suggestion, it seems, more because it would bring him home from Washington than because it would enhance his power. In February he wrote to Uncle Sardis, "I have no ambition for congressional reputation and influence, not a particle. . . . If the nomination [for Governor] is pretty likely, it would get me out of this scrape, and after that I am out of political life decently." He talked of serving a single term as Governor, then retiring to the tranquility of private law practice.

He got the nomination, and traveled tirelessly through Ohio, delivering eighty-one speeches. His combination of military heroism and quiet modesty was perfect; even though Democrats outnumbered Republicans in Ohio that year, Hayes won the election, thanks largely to the votes of war veterans. During his campaign he heeded popular trends and waved the bloody shirt, attacking the rebels and upholding the rights of Negroes. "Color ought to have no more to do with voting than size," he said. And he implied that a Democratic victory would be an invitation to revive slavery. Once elected, though, Hayes left narrow politics behind. He appointed Democrats to important state jobs, refused to fire Democrats who happened to be holding such jobs when he took over, and did much to end the tensions of the postwar era. At the next election, in 1869, he was re-elected without difficulty.

Ohio had a two-term tradition for its governors, and Hayes obeyed it, leaving office in 1871 without seeking a third nomination. He needed to return to private life, anyway, for financial reasons. Since he had refused to take advantage of his official position for his own profit, as so many others were doing, he wanted to earn some money as a lawyer to support his growing family.

He stayed active in politics, though. In 1872 he campaigned for President Grant, who was then under heavy attack by the Liberal Republican reform faction of his own party. Though he felt that Grant had been something less than a satisfactory President, Hayes remained loyal. His loyalty brought him the only political defeat of his own career; he let himself be talked into running for Congress again in the 1872 elections, and lost by 1,500 votes. The voters were showing their displeasure with Republicans in general that year, and turned against many candidates for Congress, although they re-elected Grant all the same.

Hayes practiced law, earned some money, and lived comfortably for the first time in his life. He made some good investments, and early in 1874 he inherited the estate of his Uncle Sardis; he was never really a rich man, but at least now he would have no further worries about money. He was also beginning to assume the role of Ohio's leading Republican. The Democrats had won the governorship in 1873, and were in control of the state legislature too; and when on the national level they were victorious in the Congressional elections of 1874, Hayes was concerned for the future of his party. What if the Democrats took over so many seats in Congress and in the state legislatures that they were able, by legal action, to reverse the outcome of the Civil War? He had visions of slavery restored, the Negroes deprived of the vote even in non-slave states, and all the abuses of the old regime brought back to life.

So, although he was not keen on holding office again, and was uneasy about violating the third-term tradition, Hayes ran again for Governor of Ohio in 1875. It was the best thing he could do for the Republican Party, he felt.

He won by 5,500 votes, and thus recaptured an important state from the Democrats. Suddenly he was a figure of national importance. The Republicans were looking for a presidential candidate for 1876—and many of them did not want Blaine. Hayes, three times Governor of Ohio, free of personal scandal, uninvolved in the party's fierce factional disputes, distinguished by a fine military record and a decent performance in public office, seemed just the right man for the job. And so the maneuvering began; and so the secret negotiations took place in smoke-filled hotel rooms; and so it came about that the unassuming Rutherford B. Hayes became the Republican presidential nominee for 1876.

Like Hayes, Tilden was a sickly child born in a small country village. But the resemblance between the two men ends almost at that point, for Tilden, crafty, coldly intellectual, and reserved, was a very different man from his rival for the presidency.

His birthplace was New Lebanon, New York, a farm community in the hills of Columbia County. He was born in 1814; his father was a successful farmer and a frugal man, and owned a large frame house, one of the finest in New Lebanon. Undersized and troubled by illness, young Samuel was too frail to hunt or fish with the neighborhood boys, and he remained at home leafing through books on politics, history, or philosophy. From the beginning he was a somber, quiet lad. With precocious seriousness he debated questions of politics with his father, whose friend and neighbor, Martin Van Buren, was an important figure in the Democratic Party. Young Samuel saw Van Buren often, and rejoiced when, in 1828, President Andrew Jackson named "Friend Martin" to be Secretary of State.

Two years later, sixteen-year-old Samuel left home for an academy in Williamstown, Massachusetts. He planned to become a lawyer, and then perhaps to run for public office. His weak frame left him unfit for any profession more strenuous than the law, and, in any case, the law has always been the best gateway to a political career. But he spent only three months in Williamstown before returning to New Lebanon; he felt uncomfortable away from home, and his health was so poor that he could not apply himself to his studies. At home, he involved himself in a local debating society and tried to educate himself by reading his father's books.

In the spring of 1832 he left again, this time going to New York to prepare himself for entry into college. But, despite his serious nature and his lofty ambitions, he accomplished little there. He lacked the energy for sustained study. After a few months he came home, ill and discouraged. It began to seem as though he would fail to live up to the promise of his abilities.

That summer his health improved. He spent hours riding on horseback through the hills and valleys, and his family hired a private tutor for him, who drilled him in Latin and other subjects a college student would need to know. It was hard, though, to concentrate on the works of Cicero just then, for 1832 was a presidential election year, and Tilden's passionate interest in politics kept him deeply involved in the campaign. President Jackson was running for re-election, and running with him for Vice-President was Martin Van Buren. Though he was not even old enough to vote, Sam was a delegate to the county convention of the Democratic-Republicans, as the Democrats then were known. Eighteen-year-old Tilden wrote a campaign paper, calling for the election of the Jackson-Van Buren ticket, that was published in an Albany newspaper without any indication of its authorship. It was a brilliant essay, so brilliant that many people thought Van Buren himself had written it. "Whoever the author of the appeal is," one newspaper commented, "he holds an able pen."

Tilden's candidates won the election, and soon afterward the young politician was back in New York to study. This time he did well, remaining until the spring of 1834 and keeping up with his classes even while remaining active politically. A brief diary shows his careful concern for money; he kept a record of every expense—$8 for two loads of firewood, eight cents for a tin basin to wash in, 37½¢ for candles, 25¢ for three theater tickets. By mail, he stayed in touch with the Democratic organization of Columbia County, expressing his views, drawing up resolutions, writing campaign documents. Whenever he was home he took part in committee meetings and party conventions. The older Democrats of the country were certain that this extraordinary boy was marked for national greatness; some even claimed to see a future President in him.

First, however, he had to finish his education, which had been so disjointed and haphazard thus far. In June 1834 he enrolled in the freshman class at Yale. Classroom routine irked him, though, and he found little to interest him in mathematics and Greek and Latin classics, the chief subjects of study then. He finished the summer term with creditable marks and left, fatigued and unhappy. By way of refreshment he spent the autumn of 1834 campaigning for the re-election of New York's Governor William L.

Marcy. Shortly after the election the high-strung young man was making another try at going to college—this time at New York University.

He was past twenty, and his mood was an uneasy one. He came home from college in the spring of 1835, once again tired and ill, and did not return until November; by the following April he had given up again. A summer of drifting and indecision gave way to an exciting autumn: Martin Van Buren was running for the presidency. Tilden worked hard for "Friend Martin," and saw him win a clear victory over the Whig, William Henry Harrison. After the election Tilden went back to college, and this time managed to stay there for two consecutive semesters—through July 1837. With that he ended his not very notable career as an undergraduate. He had taken no diploma, and had managed no sustained work; yet somehow, largely by self-education, he had emerged into young manhood with his capable mind well trained and well stocked with information.

It was time now to begin his career in law. Late in 1837 he became a law clerk in a New York firm, and registered for classes in the law school of New York University. He applied himself as never before, struggling successfully against ill health, carrying out the duties of his clerkship, attending classes, and—as ever—taking part in Democratic Party activities. The defeat of Van Buren by Harrison in the 1840 presidential election was a grave blow to him; when the ex-President passed through New York on his way home from Washington the following March, he visited Tilden and they spent much time analyzing the reasons for the loss. Tilden now had finished his law studies and passed his bar examinations. In the spring of 1841, Samuel J. Tilden, "Attorney and Solicitor," opened an office at 13 Pine Street, New York.

His career had begun at last, after long periods of delay and doubt. Tilden's greatest weakness was his tendency to stand still for months or even years at a time, as though paralyzed by the complexities of the world. Undoubtedly his poor health had much to do with this, but it is not the only explanation; for all his brilliance and ambition, Tilden simply found it necessary from time to time to let things slide while he took stock of himself. To some, this looked like laziness. To others, it was the caution and wariness of a wise man. Either way, it meant a mysterious lack of drive and energy, often at critical moments.

Despite these traits, the young attorney was much in demand. His cool, shrewd, keenly analytical mind was able to cut through the most tangled legal problems with ease; and the political connections he had been building up in the Democratic Party since his teens were valuable to him. Many large companies employed his services. In politics he became a member of the inner circle of the party. Not yet thirty, he was considered an elder statesman of the Democrats.

In 1843 he took public office for the first time when he was appointed Corporation Counsel of New York City. This post, which paid $2,500 a year, made him the city's official lawyer. He tried twenty or thirty cases a week and sent out hundreds of legal documents every month. His term in office was marked by his concern for the common people and by his desire to root out fraud and graft in the city government; but his health threatened to give way under the heavy burdens, and he was not greatly saddened when the Whigs won the city elections in 1844 and he, along with other Democratic officeholders, was forced to resign.

He busied himself with his growing law practice and with party activity. In the fall of 1845 he ran for office for the first time, and won election to the legislature of New York State. As a State Assemblyman, Tilden helped to engineer the election of an antislavery Democrat to the United States Senate. Tilden's views on slavery then were those of a liberal northern Democrat: that Congress should not interfere with slavery where it existed in the South, but should completely prohibit it in the western territories that were soon to become states. His thoughts on the subject were most strongly expressed in 1848, after the Mexican War. The United States had acquired as a result of this war a vast stretch of territory in the Southwest, and pro-slavery Congressmen were trying to pass a law making slavery legal in the newly conquered region. This, said Tilden, was a "monstrous and revolting proposition," for slavery had "sprung from force or fraud" and had "grown up without the original authority of law." To extend slavery now, Tilden declared, "would be the greatest opprobrium of our age" and would "cover with shame those who are struggling to establish freedom throughout the world." Years later, when Tilden was running for President and seeking the votes of former slaveowners in the South, these ringing words would return to haunt him.

Year by year Tilden rose higher in the esteem of Democratic leaders. He found public office too exhausting, though, and felt that he could serve the people and his party better by remaining in private life, working for the election of the best candidates. So he left the Assembly, and declined an opportunity to run for Congress. As a lawyer-politician, he acquired a position of great power; his advice was sought on every question, and he was always ready with shrewd and well-considered ideas. His prominence as a lawyer grew, too. He was getting higher fees, and investing his money wisely; and he was becoming wealthy. His skill with investments was such that he was asked to manage the money of many friends, and he did this so capably that he made them wealthy too. Railroads, canal companies, and coal and iron mining companies became his specialties as a lawyer, and he bought stock in the soundest and best-managed of the firms whose legal work he handled.

In 1855 he was asked to enter public life again by running for Attorney General of New York State. Typically, he hesitated for weeks after the nomination was offered, and finally accepted only because he felt it was his duty. But all the political parties were split that year over the slavery issue and over other ugly questions, such as prejudice against foreigners and Roman Catholics. A great many Irish and German Catholics had come to the United States in the 1840s and 1850s, settling mainly in New York. These newcomers, poor and bewildered in their new country, found that they could gain help from the local Democratic Party, which got them jobs and houses. In return, the immigrants voted Democratic as soon as they got their citizenship papers. But the older native-born Protestant Americans feared and resented the foreigners, partly because they spoke with strange accents and did things in a different way, partly because they were taking jobs away from native-born Americans. New political parties were formed by those who wished to keep further immigrants from entering the country, and these parties drew many votes away from the Democrats. In the 1855 elections in New York State, the Know-Nothings, one of these parties of bigotry and hatred, elected most of its candidates, and Tilden went down to defeat.

After the election, though, Tilden won a great victory in the courts. His friend Azariah C. Flagg, Democratic candidate for Comptroller of New York City, had beaten a Know-Nothing candidate by just 179 votes out of many thousands cast. The Know-Nothings claimed fraud and took the case to court, arguing that a careless election inspector had added a column of votes incorrectly in one district, while another inspector had been too drunk to notice what was happening. A number of bribed "witnesses" came forward to testify that the votes had been improperly counted and that the Know-Nothing should have won.

Tilden, as lawyer for Flagg, learned that the vote tallies in that district had conveniently disappeared. Without them, he had no way of disproving the claims of the Know-Nothing "witnesses," and it looked as though Flagg would be defeated. But Tilden succeeded in reconstructing the vote by using transfer sheets and summary tallies, working backward from these to determine what the original balloting had been. Through ingenious mathematical calculations, Tilden proved that Flagg must have been honestly elected. He kept his figures a secret until the climax of the trial; then, producing them, he shattered the case of the Know-Nothings and the jury brought in a verdict in Flagg's favor within fifteen minutes. It was a personal triumph for Tilden as a lawyer, as well as a triumph for fair elections and good government. Tilden enjoyed no such triumph, though, twenty-two years later, when he was himself the victim of an election fraud.

When the tensions of the 1850s were about to erupt into the war between North and South, Tilden recognized the dangers sooner than most men. True to his nature, he believed that time and patience could solve the problem of slavery, and hoped that loss of life and property could be avoided. He was in a ticklish position as a northern Democrat, since the Democrats had come to be increasingly dominated by the pro-slavery faction, but he did what he could to bring the quarrel to a peaceful outcome. Neither Tilden nor anyone else could have achieved that; and once he saw that civil war was inevitable, he was wholeheartedly on the side of the Union. Many northern Democrats opposed the war even after the southern states had seceded. These anti-war Democrats of the North, nicknamed Copperheads, got no sympathy from Tilden. Though too old and frail at forty-seven to think of going to war himself, Tilden fully backed the Republican President Lincoln when fighting broke out. The Constitution must be defended, said Tilden; the Union must be preserved; the seceding states must not be allowed to break away.

Tilden called for high taxation to meet the costs of the war, and the issuance of special government bonds. Always the financial conservative, he advised the Lincoln Administration to take steps to protect the value of the dollar; but this went unheeded and severe wartime inflation followed. Tilden believed more strongly in the importance of the war than some Republicans. When Lincoln asked for 75,000 soldiers in the spring of 1861, Tilden said he should have asked for 500,000. "Overwhelming numbers wisely concentrated" would beat the South swiftly; and Tilden, that man of peace, hoped for a quick northern victory that would not inflict too much devastation upon the South. He correctly foresaw the tragic effects of a lengthy war that would breed everlasting bitterness among the losers. Thus he urged great sacrifices on behalf of the war effort, so that the North could bring the unhappy affair to a rapid conclusion.

He did not switch to the new Union Party, which was basically Lincoln's Republicans plus a group of pro-war Democrats. Though he remained within his own party, his patriotism was unquestionable. He challenged the Copperheads by threatening to campaign against any Democrat who opposed the war. "We cannot afford to have two wars at the same time," he said, calling on men of his own party to support Lincoln. He never took an extreme position against the South, though. Unlike the fanatic Radical Republicans, Tilden had no wish to strip the Southerners of their property and possessions; he wished to restore the Union as peacefully as possible, and disliked the tone of vindictiveness used by some Northerners. Though a leader of the patriotic War Democrats, Tilden realized that in the long run it would be wiser to treat a defeated South gently than to exploit it cruelly as the Radicals desired.

The war made an extremely rich man out of Tilden. He had invested heavily in iron mines in Michigan, and in railroads connecting the mines to the eastern manufacturing centers. The government needed metal for guns and bullets, and the profits of Tilden's mines and railroads soared. There was nothing dishonest about this, but it brought him the label of a war profiteer; in later years he was accused of sitting back and earning millions during the Civil War while other men, such as Rutherford Hayes, were doing the fighting. Tilden's patriotic support of Lincoln's war policies went overlooked by those who could see only the fortune he had made out of the national conflict.

When Andrew Johnson became President in 1865, Tilden agreed entirely with his mild policy of restoration of the South. When Johnson was fighting for his political life in 1866 against the Radical Republicans, Tilden did all he could to help him. "Will we let the Civil War end in despotism?" Tilden asked that September. "Thank God for the triumph of national unity. . . . We are threatened by the peril of anarchy. Let no man say to me that Andrew Johnson sometimes makes passionate and angry remarks, and is guilty of indiscretions. I see him rebuilding constitutional liberty."

Nothing Tilden could say or do helped the cause of the hapless Johnson. The Radical Republicans were riding high. In 1867 they pushed through the savage Reconstruction Acts that were designed to put the South under military control indefinitely. Tilden, though no lover of slavery, was dismayed to see white men deprived of the vote in the South, and illiterate former slaves turned into brand-new Republicans. He did not oppose the granting of civil rights to Negroes, but he did not think they were qualified yet to be rulers, and Reconstruction in general struck him as a cynical plot to establish permanent Republican power in the nation. In 1868, Tilden's close friend Horatio Seymour was the Democratic candidate for President. Tilden managed his campaign and made it an attack on Radical Reconstruction.

Tilden's campaign pamphlets and speeches denounced the "ruinous policy of the Radical majority of Congress" which was prolonging the agony of the war into the postwar era. "I hoped," he said, "that we might speedily restore the people of the revolted States to their true relations to the Union," but the Republicans had proved incapable of "any large, wise or firm statesmanship," had failed "to heal the bleeding wounds," and he transformed the government into "an elected despotism" that had replaced white supremacy in the South with an equally unjust black supremacy. Tilden, like nearly all white men of his day, believed that the white race formed "a higher type of mankind" and was best fitted for the burdens of government. But he objected not so much to the presence of Negroes in legislatures and courts as to the way the uneducated southern blacks were being manipulated for the benefit of the Republican Party.

Tilden's great political skills were unable to get Seymour elected to the Presidency; the voters wanted Reconstruction, and the voters wanted Ulysses S. Grant. Tilden, the practical man who had never favored wasting energy on lost causes, turned to matters closer to home: the fantastic corruption in the government of New York City.

The huge city had come under the control of William Marcy Tweed of Tammany Hall—the infamous Boss Tweed. Tweed, a massive man with a thick beard and somber, searching eyes, had begun his career of bribery in a small way in 1859, when he and two fellow Democrats paid off a Republican politician and bought the right to name their friends as election inspectors. Within four years, Tweed had begun to drain money out of the city treasury. He held the post of Deputy Street Commissioner, which allowed him to make deals with contractors who supplied road-building materials to the city. Tweed and his cohorts decreed that the contractors were to raise their prices to the city by 35 percent over a normal profit. Of this sum, Tweed kept 25 percent and paid 10 percent to another city official. As the Tweed Ring grew wealthier, it expanded its power steadily. Tweed bribed more officials, was able to extend his looting to other city departments, and "invested" some of the profits in buying the cooperation of still more officeholders. Control of the city government was assured by purchasing votes. Thousands of immigrants who could barely speak English were given citizenship and enrolled as Democrats. For a dollar or two apiece, Tweed bought their voting loyalty. Some Democrats voted two and three times, while the bribed election inspectors looked the other way. In one election, the Democratic candidate received the votes of 8 percent more New Yorkers than were listed in the whole voting population.

Tweed eventually bribed the Mayor of New York City, the Governor of New York State, the city and state legislatures, and countless minor officials. He did not bother becoming mayor or governor himself; it was simpler to pull the strings while friendly members of the ring held the high offices and danced like obedient marionettes. Tweed grew ever bolder. In 1869 all contractors doing business with the city were told to add a 100 percent overcharge to their bills and pass the extra money along to the ring. Later the fraudulent percentage went even higher. The symbol of Tweed's misdeeds was the New York County Courthouse opposite City Hall. It was supposed to be built at a cost not exceeding $250,000, but between 1864 and 1872 some $6,000,000 was spent on the building, and $8,000,000 more was paid out for mythical work supposedly done by Tweed accomplices. The bill for carpeting the courthouse alone was $4,829,426.26—enough to carpet most of the city. The plumbing contractor collected $1,508,410.89. A plasterer named Garvey billed the city for $3,500,000. The cost of forty chairs and tables was $170,729.60. All told, the Tweed Ring milked the city for at least $75,000,000 between 1868 and 1871; one historian put the total losses at more then $200,000,000.

Tilden, that austere reformer, was remarkably slow to awaken to Tweed's doings. As a Democratic leader himself, he had frequent dealings with Tammany Hall, the city Democratic organization, and it did not seem to occur to him that Tweed was benefiting unduly from his political power. The newspapers, too, left Tweed alone, mainly because reporters and editors and even publishers were being paid to ignore the ring's activities. But by 1869 Tilden knew in a general way of the frauds, and began to speak of the "decay of civic morals." Meanwhile Tweed had so deeply entrenched himself that it looked impossible to overthrow him; he had bought the entire state, it seemed, except for Sam Tilden.

Tweed, though, was going too far. He had stolen so much that the city's financial position was imperiled, and Tilden resolved to crush him. He used his position as Chairman of the State Democratic Committee to open war on Tweed in 1870. He called for the defeat of the Tweed Ring at the polls, while the Republican New York *Times* launched a series of articles exposing the Tweed thefts, and the cartoonist Tom Nast mocked Tweed with devastating effect in the pages of *Harper's Weekly.*

Gradually, Tilden gathered the support of outraged citizens, although at first it was hard to find any important leader not tainted by Tweed's bribes. Against desperate odds Tilden succeeded in puncturing the confidence of the ring. When the *Times* began to print the actual records of Tweed thefts in the spring of 1871, and the shocking story of the courthouse reached the public, Tilden's crusade gathered strength. A Council for Political Reform was organized. The Council sent investigators to City Hall and uncovered incriminating evidence against Tweed, and the members of the ring squirmed as the threat of court action emerged. The climax of Tilden's campaign came on November 2, 1871, when he addressed a meeting at New York City's Cooper Institute and said: "The million of people who compose our great metropolis have been the subject of a conspiracy the most audacious and most wicked ever known in our free and happy land. A cabal of corrupt men have seized upon all the powers of our local government and converted them, not only to the purposes of misgovernment, but also of personal plunder. It is . . . the foremost duty of every good citizen to join with his fellows in the effort to overthrow this corrupt and degrading tyranny."

Five days later, the reform candidates in New York City were swept into office by an overwhelming majority. Most of the Tweed men were defeated, although Tweed himself held onto his seat in the State Senate through fraud. Tilden had not chosen to run for a city office; instead, he ran for the State Assembly, since he regarded the state government as the next target for reform, and was elected.

Tweed and his lieutenants were faced with criminal charges as a result of Tilden's exposures. Some fled to other states, or even to Europe; Tweed was arrested, was freed on bail, escaped to California, was brought back, and in November, 1873, was found guilty on a variety of counts and was sentenced to twelve years in prison. After a year behind bars he won his freedom on a technicality, but immediately was rearrested to face trial on a different charge. Late in 1875 the deposed boss escaped from jail, going first to Cuba and then to Spain, but he was brought back and put in New York's Ludlow Street jail a few weeks after the celebrated election of 1876, which was then bringing such turmoil into the life of his old foe Tilden. Faced with unending prosecutions, Tweed agreed to testify against his associates, and produced a staggering revelation of dishonesty in government. The confessions did not win him his freedom; he died in prison in 1878, saying, "I guess Tilden and Fairchild [who assisted Tilden's crusade] have killed me at last. I hope they will be satisfied now."

The overthrow of the Tweed Ring was Tilden's most highly publicized venture thus far. The canny political leader had been forced to step into the center of events because no one else had been willing to do the work, and now it was not so easy for the aging Tilden to retire, as he desired, to his comfortable mansion, his rare books and fine wines, and his lucrative legal practice. When he went to Albany in 1873 as an Assemblyman, his friend Horatio Seymour warned him that he was tackling another grim job. "What are you going to do at Albany?" Seymour asked him. "More than half the members [of the state legislature] hate you. You can scarcely put your finger upon a clean spot in Albany."

In New York City Tilden had smashed a Democratic machine. Now he turned against Roscoe Conkling's state Republican organization. Corrupt judges were impeached at Tilden's urging; crooked officials were rooted out. As usual, Tilden moved slowly, avoiding rash haste and sometimes seeming too hesitant, too cautious. But he got results. When the time came to choose the Democratic nominee for Governor of New York in 1874, Tilden's name led all the rest.

"There are no illusions in my mind in respect to public life," he said. "I know that peace, content, and happiness are only in a private station, and it is wholly exceptional in me to do what I am doing." Running for office meant a great financial sacrifice, for he could not attend to his legal work; but he was drawn by his responsibilities. Campaigning for high office went against the grain for this aloof, rather aristocratic man, yet he forced himself through the ordeal, organizing his campaign with the skill of a general, and won by the healthy majority of 50,000 votes. On January 1, 1875, he took office.

Certainly he was known throughout the nation by now, and to

many people as far away as California he seemed the only man who could eradicate corruption in the national government. The cry was often heard, now: "Tilden for President!" When in 1875 he uprooted the Canal Ring, a gang of upstate looters who had defrauded New York State of more than $10,000,000 since 1870, the Tilden-for-President movement grew more enthusiastic. Tilden himself realized that his road drew him inevitably toward Washington now. Some men desire the presidency for the power or the glory it provides, and scheme for years to gain the White House; Tilden was that rare figure, the man who did not really want to be President but who recognized that the nation needed him. At first hesitant, he began slowly to listen to those who were urging him to run, and then to work actively to win the office. The corrupt spirit of Grantism had to be destroyed, and it was time to end the reign of the carpetbaggers in the South. The Republicans, he said, had created "the illusion of a false prosperity" founded on an "audacious system of robbery." The country would soon be ruined if the small clique of Grant-favored privileged tycoons continued to exercise the real power of the government. As for the tortured South, it needed to be freed from the heel of the Reconstructionists: "The people are beginning to think that it is time to have a real peace in the United States," Tilden said.

This was the man the Democrats had chosen to run for President in 1876—a most unusual man, a crusader for reform, a millionaire who had gained his millions honestly, a politician who loved politics but who hated the strain of seeking votes. Long ago, Governor Marcy of New York had predicted that young Sam Tilden would be President, except for his "physical stamina. It is like putting a 200 horse power engine in a . . . craft built for only 100 horse power . . . Tilden has too much mind for his body." Now the test was at hand. A little to Tilden's own surprise, the force of events had pushed him toward the presidency. His decades of service to the Democratic Party had brought him the highest honor that party could offer to anyone. No one stood between Sam Tilden and the White House except that respectable but quite ordinary man, Rutherford B. Hayes. The candidates had been chosen. The campaign was beginning. The professional politicians of both parties agreed that Tilden would probably win. Under President Tilden, the country would have clean, efficient administration at last—though it was difficult to picture this small, passionless, reserved man as President of the United States. The hearty, affable Hayes *looked* much more like a President, people said. Yet Tilden would win. It would be close, yes—but Tilden would win.

5

The Campaign Begins

Political campaigning in the United States has always been regarded as a game, and not a very clean game. The object is to win, and rules are meant to be broken. If a candidate can win without cheating, lying, buying votes, or defaming his opponent, so much the better; but the important thing is to win, and make apologies later, if at all.

The game has changed only a little since the nineteenth century. It would be a mistake to think that it is very much cleaner today than it was then; but the players are more careful about getting caught at dirty tricks. The big eye of television is watching, ready to tell the voters whenever a candidate oversteps the bounds of decency and fair play. And Americans tend to vote against the man who oversteps those bounds too flagrantly. Thus the rough stuff takes place far behind the scenes, and the struggle for power, though as vicious as ever, is covered over by an attempt at courtesy and honorable behavior.

In the time of our great-great-grandfathers the campaigns were livelier and not so dignified. The most outrageous lies were offered as truth; the most shameful appeals were made to racial and religious prejudice; the most wicked accusations of corruption were leveled at those least deserving of them. The campaign of 1876 was no exception. If anything, it was one of the most brutal political contests of a brutal era.

Hayes and Tilden both remained out of sight during much of

the campaign, letting other men do the mud-slinging for them. That was part of the tradition too. The modern "barnstorming" campaign, in which a candidate for President tries to speak to and shake hands with every voter in the nation, had not yet been invented. In the nineteenth century, those running for the presidency remained at home, occasionally addressing a small gathering from the front porch, and making few full-scale political speeches. The struggle for votes was waged in the newspapers, and through the public speeches of the candidates' supporters.

Tilden spent the months of the campaign in his New York mansion, rarely leaving it. But that does not mean he was inactive or detached from events. The library of Tilden's house became the control center of the campaign. From that room full of musty leatherbound books the Democratic nominee directed the strategy that he hoped would make him President. It was customary for a candidate to select a campaign manager to handle that task; but Tilden, by far the cleverest politician in his party, chose to be his own campaign manager. In so doing, he outsmarted himself. The political army that he constructed had no generals, only a commander-in-chief—himself—and a great many lieutenants. When the time of crisis arrived after the election, Tilden did not have enough men capable of fighting for him. None of his aides knew enough of Tilden's grand plan; none had sufficient authority to act on Tilden's behalf.

Theoretically, Tilden's campaign manager was Abram S. Hewitt, one of his closest friends and business associates. Hewitt was the son-in-law of the famous manufacturer Peter Cooper; he owned the great Cooper & Hewitt iron mill in New Jersey, and was among the nation's wealthiest men. Hewitt had put Tilden on the path to riches by leading him to invest in iron mines. The two men had worked together to overthrow Tweed, and in 1874 Hewitt had been elected to Congress. Like many reformers of the day, Hewitt was a newcomer to politics and had little knowledge of the subtle complexities of winning an election. But he was intelligent, dedicated, and loyal, and Tilden appointed him Chairman of the Democratic National Committee. His main task was to carry out Tilden's orders, not to originate tactics. Similarly, Tilden assigned half a dozen other men a small segment apiece of the campaign responsibility, while doing all the thinking and organizing himself.

He was a magnificent organizer—so thorough and efficient that his opponents pictured him as a gigantic and sinister spider, lurking in his library and spinning a vote-snaring web. Skillfully and shrewdly Tilden carried his story to the public with a masterly public-relations operation. The Newspaper Popularity Bureau that he had set up before the nominating convention was still intact; Tilden renamed it the Literary Bureau and put it to work churning out campaign material. A team of young writers produced a 750-page book describing Republican scandals and Tilden's program for reform. By the end of August thousands of copies of this volume were in circulation, and newspapers were encouraged to quote from it as they pleased. Hundreds of papers republished the lurid tales of fraud and embezzlement. The Literary Bureau also supplied pro-Tilden editorials which newspapers could run as if their own staff men had written them; news releases about the candidate's views; speeches by Democratic orators; and bales of circulars, posters, broadsides, and fliers. The nation was blanketed with printed matter supporting Samuel Tilden. A typical publication was *The Tilden Illustrated Campaign Song and Joke Book,* which sold for a dime. The front page showed a portrait of Tilden; the next displayed the American flag. Then followed fifty pages of songs and jokes. The thirteen-stanza "Hold the Fort for Tilden" began with these lines:

See the rings, the combinations,
 Whiskey, railroad, land;
Wicked schemes for peculation
 Rife on every hand.
Chorus
Hold the fort, for we are coming,
 Hear the people cry;
Wave the answer back with fervor
 By your help we'll try.

A song to the tune of *Yankee Doodle* went like this:

Sam Tilden is a gentleman,
 A true and honest man, sir
And when we call for honest work
 He's just the chap to answer.
He represents the very truths
 That we have all been drilled in,
And we couldn't have to lead us on
 A better man than Tilden.

The Literary Bureau's vocal counterpart was the Speakers' Bureau, which endeavored to keep every Tilden rally in the country supplied with orators. The bureau chiefs compiled a long list of good public speakers and arranged intricate schedules for them so they would waste as little time as possible as they moved from town to town, delivering pro-Tilden talks. Some of these were important political figures; others were philosophers, publishers, manufacturers, and other political amateurs. Tilden himself made only two public addresses during the campaign, both of them nonpolitical; he spoke at Saratoga, New York, on applied sociology, and delivered a few words at the Centennial Exposition in Philadelphia.

Of course, local Democrats had to be recruited to stir up large attendance for these rallies and the parades that accompanied them. Tilden built an astonishing network of such groups. At the beginning of July, an "Uncle Sam Union Club," was founded in Utica, New York, and soon there were six hundred such clubs in New York State alone. Across the nation Tilden-Hendricks Clubs, Tilden Clubs, and Hendricks Clubs came into being to rouse enthusiasm for the Democratic ticket. Coordinating this mass effort was Tilden's Bureau of Correspondence, whose staff worked long hours in those pre-typewriter days to answer all letters and mail out instructions.

This vast enterprise cost money, as much as a million dollars over the four months of the campaign. In the popular imagination Tilden was fantastically rich and could pay the campaign expenses out of his own pocket, but this was not so. Though he was the most successful lawyer in the country, he was worth far less than such magnates as Rockefeller or Vanderbilt. Their fortunes were counted in the hundreds of millions of dollars; Tilden had amassed some five or ten millions, which was a good deal, but not precisely the wealth of Croesus. Moreover, he felt it would be improper for a man to try to "buy" the presidency with his personal wealth—something he was accused by his enemies of doing. So Tilden's contributions to his own campaign fund came to about $100,000, no more. The rest was raised from prosperous Democrats around the land; the biggest givers were Abram Hewitt and his brother-in-law, Edward Cooper. Some very rich Democrats were less than generous, because they felt Tilden should be making a greater financial sacrifice on his own behalf, and in the end the party did not raise as much money as it needed. This proved of critical importance in the weeks just after the election, when a fat bribe could have settled the dispute over the outcome.

The Tilden campaign was well organized, but it was not particularly vicious. The Democrats knew that they had their opponents on the defensive, and it was not necessary to resort to much libel or slander; the Republican record was bad enough without Democratic exaggeration. As the candidate of reform and clean government, Tilden could hardly afford to descend to mudslinging. Therefore he objected when some of his more hotblooded supporters tried to wage an old-fashioned kind of political campaign.

One man sent Tilden a list of scandalous topics about Hayes that could be used as campaign ammunition. Tilden refused to use any of them. Among them were the charges that Hayes had stolen the pay of dead soldiers in his Civil War regiment; that he had defrauded the State of Ohio while governor; and even the fantastic notion that Hayes had shot his mother "in a fit of insanity." Some of these stories slipped into circulation despite Tilden's objections.

Where the Democratic campaign got rough was in the South. The Democrats were counting on the electoral votes of the "redeemed" southern states, and hoped to win also in the three states—Louisiana, Florida, and South Carolina—where the carpetbaggers were still in control. But the hopes of the Democrats depended on their success in dealing with the Negro vote. The Radical Republicans had given 700,000 Negroes the right to cast ballots, and, in gratitude, nearly all of them voted Republican. In the redeemed states the carpetbaggers had been deposed through campaigns of terror that kept these Negro Republicans away from the polls while white Democrats elected their candidates. Such lawlessness was necessary now to give Tilden the South, and Tilden took care to look the other way while the southern wing of his party planned its anti-Negro strategy.

Some Democratic politicians in the South made an attempt to win Negro votes by persuasion. Wade Hampton, the Democratic candidate for Governor of South Carolina, told the Negroes of his state: "We want your votes; we don't want you to be deprived of them. . . . I pledge my faith, and I pledge it for those gentlemen who are in the ticket with me, that if we are elected . . . we will observe, protect, and defend the rights of the colored man as quickly as any man in South Carolina." The Negroes listened to this, but they did not believe it. To them the Democrats were the party of slavery and the Republicans were the party of freedom, and they planned to vote accordingly. The Democrats therefore organized "White Men's Clubs" that made an open appeal to bigotry and violence. Word was passed: any Negro who tried to vote Republican in November was risking his life.

The situation in Florida was fairly calm. Florida had never had a large slave population, and so the whites were in a majority; they hoped to oust the carpetbaggers peacefully and to cast their electoral votes for Tilden. But Louisiana and South Carolina had black majorities. If all those Negroes succeeded in voting, the two states would remain unredeemed and Republican. In Louisiana, the Democrats feared Republican fraud. Tilden was warned by one of his friends in New Orleans that Republican election inspectors would do nothing to prevent Negroes from voting fifteen or twenty times apiece for the Republican ticket. Republican officials were planning to steal the election in that state, Tilden was told, and in a close contest the votes of a single state might be crucial. It would be a sad day for American liberty if "a handful of unscrupulous carpetbaggers could determine the national election." But Tilden made no attempt to stop this fraud, probably because there was nothing he could do. The voting in Louisiana would have to remain under the supervision of the local officials, corrupt as they were.

The white Democrats of Louisiana did not plan to remain idle. They would fight fraud with fraud, if necessary, to wrest their state from the carpetbaggers. And so they got ready to keep Negroes from voting by violence. In South Carolina, much the same attitude was developing. On July 8, the whites provoked a riot at the town of Hamburg, South Carolina, at which many Negroes were killed. It was a warning of what was in store for those who dared to vote in November. Two hundred white rifle clubs had been formed, with thousands of members. More riots were planned; more black men would die.

Tilden was dismayed by the organized terrorism being planned by the southern Democrats. It went against his ideals of democracy, of course. And it was hurting his campaign in other parts of the country. Every time a white Southerner shot a Negro, Northerners remembered the issues of the Civil War and resolved to vote Republican. There was growing fear in the country that a Democratic President would give the South back entirely to the whites and wipe out the accomplishments of the Civil War. To prove that he was against slavery and hostile to white terrorism, Tilden reminded the voters that he had supported Lincoln and the Republicans during the war. These assertions of patriotism did not help. His opponents simply pointed out that he had not actually fought in the war, and that he had grown rich on the wartime profits of his mines and railroads. They still accused him of secretly sympathizing with the rebels.

This forced Tilden to make stronger statements condemning the white South. He went on record opposing any cash payments to the Confederates for loss of slaves or other property, and attacked other recently proposed measures that would have favored the secessionists. But of course this hurt him in the South. The Democrats there realized that he was just another Northerner, with little desire to help them. At that point they lost interest in Tilden. It ceased to matter to them whether Tilden or Hayes was elected; they concentrated their efforts on electing Democrats to their legislatures and governorships. To the whites of Louisiana, Florida, and South Carolina, getting rid of the carpetbaggers was much more important than working to elect the man who had just disowned them, Tilden.

Tilden was trapped. If he did not denounce the rebels, he gave the North to Hayes. If he did denounce the rebels, he might be throwing away the votes of the South. But he saw no choice. He could not compromise with his own beliefs for the sake of getting the votes of ex-Confederates. Besides, he argued, if the southern Democrats disliked him, where could they turn? To Hayes? To the Republicans? To the party of the carpetbaggers? Hardly! The argument seemed like a local one. For all his political shrewdness, though, Tilden failed to see that logic and politics do not always go together. He misjudged the South, and the South robbed him of the presidency.

Hayes had no such problems. He could vilify the South all he pleased, since a Republican candidate was expected to attack the rebels at every turn. There was no need to worry about offending the whites of Mississippi, Georgia, Virginia, and other redeemed states; they would vote Democratic regardless of anything he said for or against them. Nor did he have to go out of his way to please the white voters in the unredeemed states. There he had to hope that the votes of the carpetbaggers, scalawags, and Negroes would carry him to victory.

The Republicans were free to wave the bloody shirt, then, and they bluntly assailed the Democrats as the party of treason and rebellion. In Hayes' letter accepting the nomination, he declared that he would "wipe out the distinction between North and South," which could be interpreted as meaning that he would end the military occupation of the carpetbagger-run states, but he also said that he believed the government's role was to "protect all classes of citizens in their political and private rights." The translation was that the government would defend the Negroes against the southern whites. Hayes added, "all parts of the Constitution are sacred and must be sacredly obeyed, the parts that are new no less than the parts that are old." The reference was to the Thirteenth, Fourteenth, and Fifteenth Amendments, which prohibited slavery and guaranteed the right of Negroes to vote.

These were orthodox Radical Republican statements. In his private views Hayes was much more moderate. Basically a conservative Whig, he regretted that the southern aristocracy had suffered the loss of so much valuable property in the war—including such property as slaves. In 1875, writing to his college-days friend in Texas, Hayes said, "As to Southern affairs, 'the let alone policy' seems now to be the true course," and he declared that he had "nothing but good will" toward the South. He complained to his friend about coal miners in Ohio who, by going on strike, "make war on property," and was sympathetic when the Texan replied with a talk of "similar troubles in the South ever since the war from a discontented and ignorant class" who also made "war on property."

Hayes kept these thoughts to himself, though. For purposes of winning votes he intended to follow the time-honored Republican tradition of damning the rebels. During the campaign he wrote to Blaine, with whom he was discussing political strategy, to say, "Our strong ground is a dread of a solid South, rebel rule, etc., etc. . . . It leads people away from 'hard times' which is our deadliest foe." The Panic of 1873, brought on by Republican mismanagement, would be hard to live down, Hayes knew. The way to deal with it was to smother it in noise—directed against the weakest point of the Democrats, the Negro issue.

The mastermind of Hayes' election campaign was Zachariah Chandler, Grant's Secretary of the Interior. Chandler belonged to the Stalwart wing of the party; he was a huge, big-bellied man with an imposing fringe of whiskers, who dressed in flashy clothers, bedecked himself in diamond rings and stickpins, and was widely regarded as being too fond of drinking and gambling. Chandler was energetic, sly, and totally unscrupulous, and Hayes accepted him as campaign chairman only because he had no choice. Chandler was the Stalwarts' revenge upon the reformers for nominating Hayes; even though a clean man had won the nomination, a member of the tainted inner circle would be calling the tunes. *The Nation,* a leading magazine of political criticism, commented bitterly that in the Hayes campaign "All sorts of bad characters were usefully employed in the service of a candidate of spotless reputation, under an ingenious arrangement by which he profited by their activity without incurring any responsibility for their rascality."

Zach Chandler kept Hayes out of sight most of the time, off in Ohio obscurity, while he went about the business of winning the election. The first step was to raise money. Chandler assumed that Tilden would be pouring his personal fortune into the contest; the Republicans, then, would have to collect an even greater campaign fund in order to outbribe and outpublicize the Democrats. Unlike his opposite number on the Democratic side, Abram Hewitt, Chandler did not use the gentle methods in raising this fund. Hewitt approached only a few prosperous Democrats for contributions, but Chandler drained money out of every Republican holding public office. The technique was simple: any officeholder getting paid more than $1000 a year was required to contribute to the Hayes campaign. If he refused, vengeance would descend. This was a typical letter sent to Republican appointees in Pennsylvania:

"Our books show that you have paid no heed to either of the requests of the committee for funds . . . we look to you as one of the Federal beneficiaries to help bear the burden. Two per cent of your salary is———. Please remit promptly.

"At the close of the campaign we shall place a list of those who have not paid in the hands of the head of the department you are in."

The implications were hard to ignore, and contributions came in. Naturally, the tycoons of business who had prospered during the easygoing Republican era chipped in without the need for such prodding, and the Hayes fund grew until it was several times larger than the amount collected by the Democrats.

Chandler spent the money to send Republican campaigners up and down the land, delivering scores of speeches. Congress adjounred on August 15, and soon every important Republican figure was out informing the nation about the dangers of letting the Democrats win. John Sherman told a crowd in Marietta, Ohio, that the restoration of the Democratic Party to power would mean a nullification of the entire Civil War. The new amendments to the Constitution would be ignored; the freedmen of the South would lose their rights as human beings.

Blaine, Conkling, Morton, and others were saying the same things in a much more violent way. While audiences made up largely of northern Civil War veterans—the Boys in Blue—roared their approval, the Republican speechmakers cried that Tilden's election would mean the turning over of the United States to Confederate rule. Oliver Morton declared, "The rebellion was as much a Democratic rebellion as the St. Louis convention was a Democratic convention, actuated precisely by the same feelings." Benjamin Harrison, a future Republican President, spoke of "the black flag of treason" and "the white flag of cowardice." The most fiery words came from Colonel Robert G. Ingersoll, who had delivered the blazing "plumed knight" nominating speech for Blaine at the Republican convention. Ingersoll drew huge crowds from Maine to the Mississippi River by thundering such phrases as these:

"Every man that endeavored to tear the old flag from the heavens that it enriches was a Democrat. Every man that tried to destroy this nation was a Democrat. . . . The man that assassinated Abraham Lincoln was a Democrat. . . . Soldiers, every scar you have on your heroic bodies was given you by a Democrat."

When not stirring old national hatreds, the Republicans assailed Tilden's private character. Through speeches, whispered rumors, handbills, cartoons, and pamphlets, they mounted one of the most vengeful personal attacks of an era not noted for politeness in politics. This was the table of contents of one widely circulated anti-Tilden pamphlet:

TILDEN

1. A SECESSIONIST
   His Rebel Sympathies
   He invites Civil War
   Promotes Treason
   Declares the War a Failure

2. AN ALLY OF TWEED
   Promotes Electoral Frauds
   Mr. Greeley's Letter
   The Robberies He Facilitated
   His Share in Tweed's Conventions
   How He Stood by the Ring

3. A SHAM REFORMER
   His Canal Reforms Analyzed
   Great Cry and Little Wool
   A Lying Pretense of Economy

4. A SWINDLER OF LABOR
   Michigan Shinplasters

5. A WRECKER OF RAILROADS
   The Indiana Southern
   St. Louis, Alton and Terre Haute

The slanders against Tilden fell into two categories: his Civil War record, and his link to election frauds and railroad rings. Tilden's known patriotism during the war was deliberately over-looked and he was accused of saying such things as, "This war is a perfect outrage and I will lend no assistance whatever to its prosecution." Many Americans already interpreted "Democrat" to mean "Confederate Rebel," and the fact that Tilden had been a War Democrat was ignored. He was said to have praised slavery, aided the secessionists, made possible the murder of prisoners of war at the Andersonville camp, and committed treason against the Union. The most strenuous Tilden denials did little to destroy these blatant falsehoods.

The *Times* unearthed "new rascalities of Tilden," claiming that he had drained money out of his railroads and bankrupted whole communities; that he had paid the miners of his Michigan iron mines with "shinplasters," or worthless paper money; that he had been involved in dozens of crooked business deals; and that he had connived with Boss Tweed, turning against Tweed only when it was impossible to hide the crimes of the Tweed Ring any longer. A campaign song told of "Sly Sam, the Railroad Thief." Cartoons pictured "Tweedle-dee and Tilden-dum," linking Tweed and Tilden as cronies in graft. A book called *Samuel J. Tilden Unmasked* called him a criminal, "a disgrace to the State of New York," and "a menace to the United States." The torrent of abuse was so frightful that even Roscoe Conkling, no saint himself, was shocked by some of the things his fellow Republicans were saying about Tilden. Certainly Hayes disapproved of the ugly flood of lies.

Hayes, though, was the silent man of the campaign. Muzzled by Zach Chandler, he said nothing significant to anyone. *The Nation* remarked sarcastically that "no ingenuity of interviewers was sufficient to extract from him any expressions of opinion on any topic having the remotest bearing on the presidential contest. He recognized nothing, and neither authorized nor repudiated anybody. According to the newspaper accounts he would hardly go further in political discussion than to accede to the proposition that there was a republican form of government and that this was the hundredth year of the national government."

His only public appearance was at that stamping ground of politicians, the Centennial Exposition in Philadelphia. He went there late in October for an Ohio Day celebration, and throngs of curiosity-seekers pressed close, trying to shake his hand. Hayes was alarmed and distressed by this attention, but shook hands until he was exhausted. The impression he made that day was far from striking. The New York *Times,* which had worked hard all autumn to elect him, commented in disappointment, "Truth to say, His Excellency's personal appearance was more informal than any of those who crowded to pay their respects to him, for he wore a dreadfully shabby coat and a shockingly bad hat, all brushed up the wrong way." He looked like a country doctor or the proprietor of a small-town shop. Yet at least this kindly man with his long beard and badly tailored clothes inspired trust and affection by his very ordinariness. Tilden, who was not ordinary at all, wore fine clothes in the highest style; but he shook hands with no one, and kept the public far away.

The harsh attacks on his character were disturbing to him. Month after month, Tilden knew, he was being called a hypocrite, a thief, a drunkard, a liar, a perjurer, a swindler, a counterfeiter, and worse. The presses of his Literary Bureau were kept busy pouring out denials of all this, but Tilden was aware that denials never catch up with scandalous lies. Veteran of politics that he was, he had expected the desperate Republicans to assault him this way. A storm of similar abuse had broken Horace Greeley's heart in 1872 and killed him within weeks of Election Day, but

Tilden, though he suffered and was saddened by the propaganda, endured it and kept up his own fight. He hammered away at Grantism and other species of Republican corruption, proclaimed his own program for clean and sound government, and tried to reassure the North that he would not hand the country over to the Confederates if elected.

The nation responded. This small, sickly, almost feeble man caught the popular imagination. The poor, the hungry, the oppressed, saw him as their rescuer from the political bosses and the bloated millionaires. In almost every city, torchlight parades and brass bands celebrated the coming deliverance from Republican misrule. *TILDEN AND REFORM,* the banners cried. Tilden was a most unlikely hero—but a hero he was.

Behind the hysteria of the campaign were practical men, calculating the chances. It was not the popular vote that mattered so much as the electoral vote, thanks to the system handed down by the nation's founders. The voters would not be casting ballots for Hayes or for Tilden. They would be voting for *electors*— prominent men picked by the parties. The number of each state's electors was the total of its Senators and Representatives: New York had 35, Florida 4, California 6, Michigan 11. This reflected the populations of the states, for, while each state had two Senators, the number of Representatives was allotted according to population figures.

The voters in each state, then, would choose between a set of Democratic electors pledged to Tilden, and a set of Republican electors pledged to Hayes. The party getting the most votes in a state would take all of that state's electoral votes. On December 6, the successful electors would meet to choose the President. That year there were 369 electors in all, so 185 electoral votes would be needed to win.

Many things can go wrong using this system, which is still in effect. Nothing in the Constitution prevents an elector from voting as he pleases—for an elector pledged to the Democratic candidate to vote for the Republican, or vice versa. This has happened a few times. Then, too, it is possible for a candidate to win a majority of the electoral votes while getting less than a majority of the popular votes. This can come about if he wins extremely close elections in the states with many electoral votes—New York, Ohio, Pennsylvania, and Illinois, for example—while losing by a wide margin in thinly populated states like Wyoming, Nevada, Utah, and Montana. Winning by a single vote in New York is worth more than winning by millions of votes in a dozen western states put together.

The strategy of a wise candidate is to concentrate on the states with many electoral votes, since they hold the key to victory. Tilden, as Governor of New York, was almost certain to carry his own state, and he believed he would win in neighboring New Jersey and Connecticut. Those three alone would give him 50 of the needed 185 electoral votes. He expected most of the New England and the Middle West to vote for Hayes, as well as the Far West. Ohio, Minnesota, Kansas, Massachusetts, Pennsylvania, Colorado, and Nevada all looked lost to the Democrats. But Tilden anticipated doing well in the eight Confederate states that had returned to white rule—Virginia, North Carolina, Georgia, Alabama, Tennessee, Mississippi, Arkansas, and Texas. These states had 76 electoral votes. He was sure of Virginia, North Carolina, Tennessee, and Texas, where white voters were in the majority. Georgia, Alabama, and Mississippi were more doubtful, because so many Negro Republicans had been placed on the voting lists during Reconstruction. Louisiana, South Carolina, and Florida, the remaining carpetbagger states, were more doubtful yet. It he got at least the 76, though, he would need only 59 more electoral votes, and he hoped to gain them in such border states as Missouri, Kentucky, Maryland, Delaware, West Virginia, and Indiana. Most observers thought that Tilden would indeed scrape through by eight or ten electoral votes. Among New York gamblers, the odds were five to two in favor of his election.

The first solid clue to the direction the voters might take came on October 10, when Ohio and Indiana held elections for state offices. The results were encouraging to the Democrats. They had not bothered to campaign hard in Ohio, which was Hayes' state; but Ohio went Republican in October by only 6,600 votes. Tilden realized that he stood a fair chance of taking Ohio away from Hayes—and winning the election. Indiana, the home state of Senator Hendricks, Tilden's running mate, went Democratic even though many Indianans disliked Tilden's financial theories.

The outlook was good for the presidential election on November 7. Many uncertainties remained, though. The South in particular was unpredictable. Almost anything might happen there in the final weeks of the campaign. Tilden feared some last-minute move by the Republicans that would upset the voters and disrupt his pattern of victory—and his fears were justified.

6

———— ⟫⟪◉⟫⟪ ————

The Nation Chooses

Taking stock of the election situation in mid-October, the Republican leaders admitted that things looked bad for Hayes. If Tilden carried New York and its neighboring states, Indiana, and the entire South, he would be President. The Hayes men sought some way of prying loose some southern electoral votes for their candidate.

The place to look was the three carpetbagger states ruled by Republican governors. If these states could somehow be shifted into the Republican column on November 7, Hayes might win. But how? The whites of Louisiana, South Carolina, and Florida were determined to redeem their states this year. They were applying force to keep Negro Republicans away from the polls. Only through greater force could the Redeemers be defeated.

That was the answer: send in government troops! Use brigades of soldiers to decide the outcome of the election!

There had been racial trouble in South Carolina all summer. Massachusetts-born Daniel H. Chamberlain, the eloquent and conscientious Republican governor, had been unable to keep order. Thousands of armed whites belonging to rifle clubs roamed the state, systematically terrorizing Negro voters. The Negroes returned the violence, particularly in the eastern part of the state, where Negro field hands were on strike against the rice plantations for higher wages. Bands of these laborers harassed the nonstriking workers and attacked whites at random. The fact that the

Democrats had nominated a former Confederate general, Wade Hampton, to run against Chamberlain for governor, did not make matters less tense.

On September 16 there came a bloody collision between the races at the town of Ellenton. Other riots followed, and law and order broke down entirely in South Carolina. As chaos threatened, Governor Chamberlain asked President Grant to send Federal soldiers to restore peace in the troubled state.

Under similar circumstances, in 1875, Grant had refused to send troops to Mississippi, because it seemed politically unwise for him to extend the military suppression of the southern whites. Thus Mississippi had been redeemed. But now it was a presidential election year, and the Republicans were aware that if they lost South Carolina they would lose the election. Grant weighed all the political risks and dispatched the troops. On October 17, 1876, he issued a proclamation of insurrection and ordered thirty-three companies of Federal soldiers into South Carolina. This was nearly the whole defense force for the Atlantic seaboard. The soldiers spread out through the state in small squads and brought the rioting to an end.

Two weeks before Election Day, South Carolina was thus under full military occupation. The occupying soldiers were Northerners and Civil War veterans, mainly—which meant they were Republicans. They knew they had not been sent merely to keep order, but to watch over the presidential election. On October 19 *The Nation* expressed its fear that "the soldiers . . . who are now making arrests for 'intimidation' in South Carolina, and who are to preserve order at the polls on Election Day, are really an armed force in the service, and acting under the orders of, one of the parties to the political contest." Judge Walter Gresham of Indiana, an independent Republican, wrote to a friend on October 24 to express his anger at the use "of bayonets in connection with the election . . . a dangerous thing. I am afraid of such precedents. How long will it be before the same thing is resorted to in the North!" He was disturbed by the possibility that Hayes would be fraudulently "counted in" by armed might. *The Nation* observed that the Republicans were planning to use the Army "either for physical interference or moral influence on their side." Law-abiding Americans of both parties watched the developments with uneasiness. What if Tilden won the election fairly, they asked, and were deprived of his office by force? Would that not split the nation in a new Civil War? The country that had just celebrated its one hundredth birthday was in a grim mood as Election Day drew near.

The voters went to the polls on Tuesday, November 7. *I am looking anxiously forward to the end of the contest,* Hayes had written in his diary, and most of the country felt the same way. A Tilden victory was still predicted; *The Nation* thought he would win every southern state except South Carolina, plus Indiana, New York, and a few other northern states. But no one knew what might happen afterward. A close election might spark revolution if the Republicans refused to let go of the White House.

Voting was heavy. Democrats determined to bring about reform, Republicans equally determined to keep control of the presidency, streamed to the polls. The troops in South Carolina prevented disorder by keeping black men from voting. In Louisiana, mobs of white men and mobs of Negroes wandered the streets, shouting, looting, fighting. There were illegalities on both sides, particularly in the South. Men voted ten and twenty times apiece; local bosses stood by the ballot boxes to dictate the choice of candidates; votes for the wrong man were torn up and thrown away.

Governor Hayes voted on a raw, disagreeable day in Ohio, and retired to his home in Columbus to wait for the returns. In New

York, Governor Tilden cast his ballot in the morning, then visited Democratic headquarters at noon, and went home about four o'clock. For the rest of the day, dressed in black with a red flower in his buttonhole, he received visitors. He was dignified but quietly confident. Despite a cold rain, a crowd of cheering people gathered outside his Manhattan home, straining to catch a glimpse of the man who was going to be President.

The polls closed at sundown and the counting began. A network of telegraph operators was ready to transmit the returns. Radio and television, of course, were unknown then; the telephone was still crude and imperfect. Great bulletin boards were posted outside courthouses, party headquarters, and other places where returns were being tallied; as each batch of figures came over the telegraph lines, the new totals were chalked outside or read aloud to the waiting groups of citizens.

The early returns from New York City showed Tilden far ahead, but that was no surprise. The figures from upstate New York also gave Tilden the lead—more significant, since the upstaters were mostly Republicans. Perhaps the rainy weather had kept the Republican farmers at home; or perhaps New Yorkers of both parties hoped to see a New York man in the White House. New York's big bloc of 35 electoral votes was going to Tilden, that was certain. Connecticut and New Jersey were going to the Democrats also. Now the Indiana votes were coming in—and they showed Tilden and Hendricks with a safe lead over Hayes and Wheeler. After dinner, Tilden went to the Democratic headquarters to follow the returns, and in late evening a sense of quiet triumph spread through the room. Tilden had won the key northern states which, added to the certain southern states, would give him the presidency.

A procession of messenger boys brought the returns to Hayes, who was surrounded by a small group of friends at his home. The gloom deepened there as the evening wore on. Hayes had needed New York and Indiana for victory; once it was certain that they were lost, it looked like a Tilden landslide. News came to Hayes that he had carried his home state of Ohio. He had won in New Hampshire, Vermont, Massachusetts, Rhode Island, and Illinois. Michigan was his, and so were Pennsylvania, Wisconsin, Iowa, Kansas, Nebraska. The first figures from the West told him that he was leading in California, Nevada, and Oregon. But what did that matter? If Tilden took the South, he had the election. And Tilden was taking the South.

The trend was unclear in the carpetbagger states. South Carolina, with the help of Federal troops, seemed to be going to Hayes, but Louisiana and Florida appeared to be backing Tilden. Even before the polls had closed, though, each side had claimed widespread fraud, and no one could be sure what the outcome would be. In the redeemed states, however, Tilden was far ahead and piling up an impressive total of electoral votes. Virginia, North Carolina, Georgia, Alabama, Mississippi, Arkansas, Tennessee, and Texas were his. So were the border states: Kentucky, Missouri, West Virginia, Maryland, Delaware. Tilden would win the election even if he lost two of the three carpetbag states to the Republicans.

Tilden went to bed about midnight, thinking he had been elected. Hayes, too, felt that the election had been decided in favor of the Democrats. He had thought so since learning that Tilden had carried New York. *From that time,* he noted in his diary, *I never supposed there was a chance for Republican success.* Jubilant Democrats paraded in the streets. Sounds of gay laughter drifted through the darkness. Even in the rain, huge bonfires blazed. The New York *Tribune,* a Republican paper, declared in its first edition Wednesday morning that Tilden had been elected. The New York *Evening Post* calculated that Tilden had 209 electoral votes, Hayes 160. But the New York *Herald* was less certain. Its headline was THE RESULT—WHAT IS IT? SOMETHING THAT NO FELLOW CAN UNDERSTAND. IMPOSSIBLE TO NAME OUR NEXT PRESIDENT. THE RETURNS TOO MEAGER. Yet the *Herald* believed that Florida, Louisiana, and Oregon would go to Tilden when all votes were tallied, and noted, "Returns seem to indicate that Governor Tilden has been elected."

Only the New York *Times* refused to concede Hayes' defeat. The *Times* was a bitterly pro-Republican paper, and its managing editor, John C. Reid, had personal reasons for hating the Democrats. Reid had suffered in a Confederate prison during the Civil War, and he regarded all Democrats as rebels and therefore as demons. Reid had glumly watched the demons win the election that night, but in the dark hours of the night he and a few other men invented a bold scheme for turning defeat into victory.

About midnight on Election Day the Democratic National Chairman, Abram Hewitt, had sent a message to the *Times* asking what size majority it felt Tilden had won. Reid replied defiantly, "None!" At that time his response was pure bravado, for even he believed that Tilden had won by a close margin. When the *Times* editors gathered soon afterward to plan the morning's edition, they debated the approach to take, and decided simply to print a story saying that the outcome was in doubt. At 3:45 A.M., before the paper had gone to press, they received a startling message from Dan Magone, Chairman of the State Democratic Committee: PLEASE GIVE YOUR ESTIMATE OF ELECTORAL VOTES SECURED FOR TILDEN. ANSWER AT ONCE. The astonished *Times* editors realized that things were even closer than they had thought. The Democrats themselves did not know who had won—and were naïvely trying to find out if the *Times* had the latest returns!

Magone's foolish admission of doubt gave Reid his chance. If the Democrats did not have definite news of the final votes, perhaps it might not be too late to manipulate those votes. Reid checked through the figures and saw that nothing final had come in from Louisiana, South Carolina, or Florida. The Democrats appeared to be ahead in two of those states, but no matter; Republican officials would be in charge of certifying the tally. If they could distort the returns enough to throw Florida and Louisiana to Hayes, the Republicans would win the election!

Reid rushed to the Fifth Avenue Hotel, where the Republicans had set up their campaign headquarters. Most of the party workers had gone off dejectedly to sleep; when Reid arrived, he found only one member of the committee, William E. Chandler. Chandler, a small man wearing an immense overcoat, was morosely reading the New York *Tribune*'s account of Tilden's victory. Reid assured him that all would turn out well "if you keep your heads up here."

Breathlessly Reid produced the list of election returns, showed how close the election had been, and pointed out what would happen if Hayes were to be pronounced the winner in Florida and Louisiana.

"What should be done?" Chandler asked.

"Telegraph immediately to leading Republicans," said Reid.

"We must go and see Zach," Chandler replied. He was referring to his namesake, Zach Chandler, the bulky, hard-drinking Republican National Chairman. Together they went upstairs to wake up the chairman.

Zach Chandler, clad in his nightshirt, blinked and yawned and rubbed his eyes and tried to comprehend what Reid was telling him. Befuddled by sleep and liquor, he could barely understand the electoral arithmetic at first. Slowly Reid's urgent flow of words sank in. Reid spelled out his plan, and Zach Chandler said drowsily, "Go ahead and do what you think necessary."

Reid and William Chandler sped off to the main office of Western Union and began composing telegrams. The one sent to Governor Chamberlain of South Carolina declared:

HAYES IS ELECTED IF WE HAVE CARRIED SOUTH CAROLINA,
FLORIDA, AND LOUISIANA. CAN YOU HOLD YOUR STATE? ANSWER
IMMEDIATELY!

Similar telegrams went to Republican chieftains in Florida and
Louisiana. For good measure Chandler also wired party leaders
in Oregon and California, where votes were still being counted.
The instructions were the same: HOLD YOUR STATE. What that
meant, simply, was that all means were to be used, whether legal
or not, to deliver the state to Hayes. The situation was critical;
quick action might yet snatch the election from Tilden. All depended now on how firmly the carpetbaggers controlled the three
vital southern states. Could they interfere with the election returns? Could they throw out Democratic votes and make it seem
as if Hayes had won?

The telegraph operator believed the Republicans had lost, and
therefore refused to let the telegrams be charged to the Republican National Committee—knowing that defeated politicians
rarely paid their bills. Angrily, Reid told the man to charge the
telegrams to the *Times*. Then he headed back to the newspaper
office to continue the process of stealing the election.

The first November 8 edition of the *Times* was already on sale.
It carried this editorial:

A DOUBTFUL ELECTION

> At the time of going to press with our first edition
> the result of the presidential election is still in doubt.
> Enough has been learned to show that the vote has
> been unprecedently heavy . . . and that in some of the
> States where the shotgun and rifle clubs were relied
> upon to secure a Democratic victory, there is only too
> much reason to fear that it has been successful.

The second edition, which appeared at 6:30 A.M., advanced the
conspiracy to the next stage. Reid gave Louisiana, South Caro-

lina, and Oregon—all doubtful states—to Hayes. The *Times* thus awarded 184 electoral votes, one short of a majority, to Tilden, and 181 electoral votes to Hayes, with Florida's four votes still in doubt. In the next edition the *Times* claimed Florida for Hayes, making him the winner of the election, 185 to 184.

Zach Chandler was awake by then. He had already received secret telegrams from the Republican campaign managers in Louisiana and Florida telling him that the Democrats had won in those states. Chandler quietly threw the telegrams away and went by the totals the *Times* had audaciously manufactured. That morning Chandler announced:

"Hayes has 185 electoral votes and is elected."

Claiming victory was one thing; making the claim stick was something else again. Zach Chandler had to see to it that his carpetbagger allies in the South cooperated fully in the fraud. In each state, the decision rested with an official body called a "returning board," whose job it was to examine the election returns, check the count, disqualify any votes obtained through illegal means, and certify the winner. In South Carolina and Louisiana, the returning boards were composed entirely of Republicans; in Florida, the board consisted of one Democrat and two Republicans. What Chandler wanted the returning boards to do was to juggle the figures to show a majority for Hayes. This would take some doing; in Louisiana, for example, Tilden had won by a majority of almost 9000 votes out of 207,000. The returning board would have to throw out 10 percent of the Democratic ballots to give the state to Hayes.

It was a risky business, but the stakes were high. Chandler knew he could make Hayes President only by buying the loyalty of the returning boards, and this he was prepared to do. The day after the election, he sent William Chandler to the South to hand out payments to the key people. Zach Chandler was ready to pay not only in cash but in political power. He wrote to one returning-board member, "The election of Hayes depends on Florida. W. E. Chandler has gone to Florida to see you with full powers to act and make terms. You can put a man in the Cabinet or elsewhere if you choose to demand it. Do so and get a friend where he can help you. Don't be modest. Agree to carry the state . . . and you can have your own terms in your hands."

While these maneuvers were going on, the Democrats were waking after their victory celebrations to discover that strange things had happened in the night. One of Tilden's campaign managers wired from Pennsylvania: IS THERE ANY DOUBT? ALL SORTS OF REPORTS HERE. The Democratic National Committee was bombarded with questions, but had no answers. Tilden, after a late breakfast, walked to the party headquarters and conferred with his lieutenants. They agreed that the situation was troublesome, but still believed they had won, despite the strident claims of the *Times*. When he returned home in the early afternoon, Tilden graciously accepted the cheers of people who saw him in the streets, and told a reporter for the *World*, "My election was due . . . to the issues. . . . I received a great number of Republican votes. . . . The election was decided in part on my record as governor." That evening he entertained forty persons at a victory dinner in his home.

Hayes, far removed from the center of political action and unaware of the activities of Zach Chandler and John Reid, issued a dignified statement of defeat during that day: "I don't care for myself; and the party, yes, and the country, too, can stand it; but I do care for the poor colored men of the South. . . . The result will be that the Southern people will practically treat the constitutional amendments as nullities, and then the colored man's fate will be worse than when he was in slavery."

A little later on Wednesday, Hayes learned in amazement that

Zach Chandler was claiming victory for him. He remained calm, and was rather skeptical of his chances. The *Ohio State Journal* reported the next day that Hayes "received those who called in his usual cordial manner and was very unconcerned while the greatest office on the American continent was trembling in the balance." He told a reporter for a Cincinnati newspaper, "I think we are defeated in spite of recent good news. I am of the opinion that the Democrats have carried the country and elected Tilden." These comments annoyed Chandler considerably. If Hayes' election depended on white southern support, this was no time for him to bemoan the fate of "the poor colored men." And Chandler would hardly be able to swing the doubtful states into the Republican column if Hayes kept on admitting defeat. Abruptly Hayes stopped making public statements.

Tilden, too, had nothing to say to reporters, keeping cool and quiet while he assessed the turn of events. The New York *Herald,* a couple of days after the election, spoke of Tilden's "wonderful self-control" and said he displayed "no anxiety." The article described the Democratic candidate as "A most accomplished and astute politician—less confiding and more distrustful than Grant—a man of modest, unobtrusive personality . . . stooped and hence looks smaller than he is—small smooth boyish face—round head bent with that sleepy droop in the left eyelid . . . so weak, so mild, so selfless, so uncombative . . . surrounded by political giants who bow before the modest little man with the cold, passionless, sagacious face. . . ."

The "political giants," and the ordinary citizens as well, were growing increasingly more perturbed as the complexities of the election unfolded. The New York *Herald* on November 9 headed election news with NECK AND NECK! WHO IS IT? and credited Tilden with 184 votes, Hayes 151, leaving 34 in doubt. A day later the *Herald* said that Tilden still had 184 votes, Hayes 166, and 19 were uncertain. Most Republican papers now had joined the *Times* in insisting that Hayes had been elected. The Democratic journals continued to claim a Tilden victory. All the votes had by now been counted, but no one was sure which set of totals to accept. In the three disputed southern states, the Republicans controlled the state governments and the election machinery, and appeared to be producing fraudulent returns. But the Democrats had openly waged a campaign of threats, intimidation, and even violence to keep Negroes from voting. Which was more honest—a Republican victory brought about by dishonest counting, or a Democratic victory brought about by preventing voters from casting their ballots?

This was the way the count looked on November 10:

HAYES		TILDEN	
California	6	Alabama	10
Colorado	3	Arkansas	6
Illinois	21	Connecticut	6
Iowa	11	Delaware	3
Kansas	5	Georgia	11
Maine	7	Indiana	15
Massachusetts	13	Kentucky	12
Michigan	11	Maryland	8
Minnesota	5	Mississippi	8
Nebraska	3	Missouri	15
Nevada	3	New Jersey	9
New Hampshire	5	New York	35
Ohio	22	North Carolina	10
Oregon	3	Tennessee	12
Pennsylvania	29	Texas	8
Rhode Island	4	Virginia	11
Vermont	5	West Virginia	5
Wisconsin	10		184
	166		

IN DOUBT

Florida	4
Louisiana	8
South Carolina	7
	19

Hayes had carried 18 states; Tilden had taken 17, including most of those with large populations. Three were uncertain. (There were only 38 states in the Union in 1876; the territories, such as Idaho, Wyoming, New Mexico, and Utah, were not allowed to vote in the national election.) So far as the popular vote went, Tilden was clearly ahead; the final figures showed that he led Hayes by 4,300,000 votes to 4,036,000, a majority of better than a quarter of a million. But American presidential elections are not decided on the basis of the popular vote; and the electoral vote totals as of November 10 showed Tilden one vote short of a majority. Even so, his position was far from grave. If he could squeeze out only a single vote from the three undecided states, he would be President. Even if he lost all three to the Republicans, he might still win if just one elector of independent opinions switched his vote from Hayes to Tilden, as the electors had the privilege of doing when they met to cast their votes in December.

"The fiery zealots of the Republican Party may attempt to count me out," Tilden remarked on the third day after the election, "but I don't think the better class of Republicans will permit it." Nevertheless, the Democrats were so distressed that they conceived a diversionary tactic to secure Tilden's one needed elector. Hayes had carried Oregon; but one of the Republican electors, J. W. Watts, was found to be a postmaster. The Constitution declares that "no Senator or Representative, or Person holding an Office of Trust or Profit under the United States, shall be appointed an Elector." On November 15, Tilden's campaign manager, Abram Hewitt, sent a telegram to Governor L. F. Grover of Oregon, pointing out that Postmaster Watts, as a government official, was disqualified from serving as an elector. Grover, who was a Democrat, agreed. He voided the election of Watts and declared that E. A. Cronin, a Democratic elector, would be allowed to cast one of Oregon's three electoral votes. This maneuver took away a vote that the people of Oregon wished to cast for Hayes, and awarded it on a technicality to Tilden.

The other two Republican electors refused to meet with Cronin. Watts resigned his postmastership and claimed to be the legally chosen third elector; he met with the other two Republicans and they cast three electoral votes for Hayes. Governor Grover appointed two more Democrats to replace the balky Republicans; they convened with Cronin and declared that Oregon cast two electoral votes for Hayes and one for Tilden. The governor signed this vote, certifying it as official. Both sets of votes were forwarded to Washington to be counted. Hewitt admitted that Tilden had no real right to Oregon's vote, and that the claim to it was merely intended "to offset the palpable frauds in Florida and Louisiana." The effect of the maneuver was to throw doubt on yet another state's vote—and no one knew how to untangle the growing confusion.

While this Oregon operation was going on, the nation's attention was centered on Florida, Louisiana, and South Carolina, where the returning boards were meeting to rule on the disputed votes. Politicians of both parties were heading southward to keep an eye on the proceedings. Some of them were there for shady purposes, such as William Chandler, who had sped to Florida the day after the election to distribute Republican cash and promises of high offices to the talliers of the vote. The Democrats were quick to get their own secret agents into the South. Bribes would have to be countered by bribes, whether the high-minded Tilden liked it or not. A Democratic leader in Florida wired Tilden, NEED

MONEY TO RESIST RADICALS PRANKS. And Henry Watterson, one of Tilden's chief aides, telegraphed the candidate, OUR FRIENDS IN LOUISIANA NEED MORAL SUPPORT AND PERSONAL ADVISEMENT, by which he meant money. A STRONG DEMONSTRATION WILL DEFEAT THE DESIGNS OF THE RETURNING BOARD, BECK, MCHENRY AND I START TONIGHT, YOU MUST REINFORCE US. Tilden was unwilling to authorize bribery, but he gave permission for some of his men to make what arrangements they could in the South.

Not all the politicians who went there were bent on connivance, though. On November 8, Abram Hewitt had suggested that a committee of eminent citizens go to South Carolina, Louisiana, and Florida to see that "a fair count was made, and the returns honestly canvassed." The Republicans quickly agreed that this should be done. Platoons of important Democrats and Republicans, designated as "visiting statesmen," were chosen to keep their eyes on the activities of the returning boards. The Republican visiting statemen included such loyal Hayes men as John Sherman and Edward Noyes, and also Representative James A. Garfield, a future President. The Democrats sent a variety of prominent men who had been active in Tilden's campaign.

Despite the presence of the visiting statesmen—or even because of it—the possibility of fraud and disorder remained great. The visitors might well succeed in putting such pressure on the returning boards that the outcome of the election might be swayed in some unpredictable direction. President Grant, the forgotten man in all this excitement, took steps to insure that, no matter what, the Republicans would remain in control of things. On November 10 he ordered a further contingent of troops sent into the three southern states, "to preserve peace and good order, and to see that the proper and legal Boards of Canvassers [the returning boards] are unmolested in the performance of their duties." He placed these troops under the command of General William Tecumseh Sherman, one of the North's greatest Civil War heroes—and the brother of Hayes' chief supporter, Senator John Sherman of Ohio. Any violence that might be harmful to the Republican cause would meet swift suppression.

The visiting statesmen introduced a new note of tension into the crisis. They were the shrewdest and most powerful politicians in the country, and as they jockeyed for influence they created conflicts and doubts among the men responsible for tallying the votes. No one could predict what the result would be, not even the visiting statesmen themselves. John Sherman wrote to a friend on November 12, "Now that the election is over results are as uncertain as before. . . . I have been invited by the President to go to New Orleans . . . but I see no good to come of it." Sherman believed that white intimidation of Negro voters in the South had succeeded in electing Tilden. Two weeks later, Sherman wrote from New Orleans that he now felt Hayes would be the winner, but that "It is a dangerous ending of our . . . contest to have it decided by the . . . doubtful votes of three States where fraud, murder, and violence have prevailed for years. I have got the insight into the history of politics here that alarms me for the peace of the whole country."

7

The Struggle for Votes

A baffled nation watched as the southern returning boards began their work in mid-November. Many leaders of both parties were privately convinced that Tilden had been elected—but the returning boards had the power to undo that. Tilden received a flood of letters and telegrams offering sympathy and support. Such a powerful Republican as Senator Roscoe Conkling declared that he believed Tilden had won, and offered "hearty cooperation." Conkling was less noble than it might seem in this; having lost the nomination to Hayes, he was embittered enough to want to see Tilden the winner, even at the expense of his own party.

Tilden remained far above the struggle—remote, detached, hardly seeming to care what was going on. He held endless conferences with his campaign managers, but never arrived at a course of action. One Congressman wrote to him to suggest seizing the presidency by force if the Republicans attempted fraud. "Nerve and resolution will win for you," he said. But Tilden showed neither nerve nor resolution, in the eyes of his most loyal followers. He chose to bide his time and rely on the Constitution, believing that his cause was just and that justice would triumph. It was a strangely naïve attitude for such an experienced politician, but it was honorable. Honor was a scarce commodity that year.

So Tilden remained silent for reasons of honor, and his impatient friends thought he was a procrastinator, paralyzed by the crisis and unable to act. Tilden refused to bribe, and some of his friends said he was stingy. He was offered the electoral votes of South Carolina for $80,000, and turned the deal down, even though he knew that the Republicans were "bidding high" for the presidency.

Hayes, too, managed to stay clean during the undignified hunt for electoral votes. Ignorant of the deceit and fraud being practiced on his behalf, Hayes remained in Columbus, Ohio, watching the unfolding events in concern and mystification. When John Sherman sent him a report on the situation late in November, Hayes replied, "A fair election would have given us about forty electoral votes in the South—at least that many. But we are not to allow our friends to defeat one outrage and fraud by another. There must be nothing crooked on our part. Let Mr. Tilden have the place by violence, intimidation and fraud, rather than undertake to prevent it by means that will not bear the severest scrutiny."

The Constitution provided that the presidential electors should meet on the same day throughout the nation in their individual states and cast ballots for President and Vice-President. The ballots, signed and certified, were to be sealed and sent to Washington, where they would be opened and counted by the President of the Senate in the presence of the Senate and the House of Representatives. Since the elections in the three southern states were so close, though, no one knew whether the Democratic or Republican electors had won the right to cast ballots. That was what the returning boards had to decide.

The problem of the South Carolina vote was the least complicated. President Grant had filled the state with Federal troops two weeks before the election, and the soldiers had seen to it that few Negro voters were kept from the polls. The result was a small but definite majority for Hayes. The returning board consisted of seven members, all Republicans; three were Negroes. The board had the power "to decide all cases under protest or contest." The only chance the Democrats had to win in South Carolina was by bribing these seven Republicans to award the state to Tilden. Smith M. Weed, a Democratic agent, visited the board members and asked their price. He was told at first that it would cost $75,000 to get two or three of the state's electoral votes; by brisk negotiating he arranged to buy all seven for $80,000, and hurried to New York to get the money from Tilden. Tilden, of course, refused to pay, and the scheme collapsed.

The Democrats in South Carolina continued to press their shaky case. They turned now to the Supreme Court of South Carolina, which also was made up of Republicans, and wangled a court order preventing the returning board from reaching an immediate decision. A few days of stalemate followed; then the returning board awarded the state's electors to Hayes, and the court approved.

Trouble was developing, though, over South Carolina's contest for the governorship. Wade Hampton, the Democratic candidate for governor, had apparently been elected by a few thousand votes over Republican Governor Chamberlain. The state legislature had the right to make the final decision in a disputed gubernatorial election—but the makeup of the legislature itself was in doubt. Amid great frenzy, *two* legislatures were sworn into office, one dominated by Democrats, one led by Republicans. The Republican legislature voted to keep Chamberlain; the Democratic legislature decreed that Hampton had been elected. In December 1876 both governors were duly inaugurated. Protected by Federal troops, Chamberlain occupied the state capitol. Hampton sent up a capitol-in-exile elsewhere in the city of Columbia, and was recognized by most whites as the legitimate governor.

Who was really Governor of South Carolina, though? No one knew—and an unsavory political deal began to take form. The white Democrats of South Carolina were concerned with redeeming their state from the carpetbaggers much more than they were with electing Tilden. They hardly cared about Tilden at all; he was a Northerner, and most of his philosophy was alien to them. The important thing was to get rid of Republican governors in South Carolina.

So the South Carolina Democrats quietly began to talk business with a few of Hayes' visiting statesmen. They offered to withdraw their claim to South Carolina's electoral votes on Tilden's behalf—provided the future President Hayes would recognize Wade Hampton as the rightful governor, and remove Federal troops from their state. It was a way of buying South Carolina's redemption, a way of getting a Democratic governor at the expense of having a Republican President. The National Democratic Party knew nothing about this arrangement.

On December 6, the day the electors cast their ballots, South Carolina turned in two sets, one certified by Chamberlain for Hayes, one certified by Hampton for Tilden. Having failed to carry the state for Tilden, the national Democrats hoped now to get the entire South Carolina vote thrown out because of fraud, thus keeping the seven electoral votes away from Hayes' column. Congress would have to decide the question of which set of electoral votes to accept.

It was generally admitted that Hayes had really carried South Carolina, thanks to the presence of the soldiers; the only problem there was the one raised by the Democratic electors who claimed, without much justification, that they had won. Tilden's case was flimsy there at best. But matters were harder to decide in Florida. The state had a majority of white voters, but its government was still in the hands of carpetbaggers. The Democrats had used intimidation to keep Negro Republicans from voting, and the Republicans had used fraud to discard Democratic votes. The two illegalities just about balanced each other out, and the crooked election was virtually a draw. When all the votes were in, the Democrats claimed that Tilden had won the state by 93 votes. The Republicans said that Hayes was the winner by 45 votes. The returning board would have to decide the election. The board consisted of a carpetbag Republican, a scalawag Republican who had deserted the Confederate Army, and a Democrat.

The reputations of these three men were such that they might go either way. Normally, the board could be expected to vote for Hayes, 2–1. But an injection of cash might serve to change the views of one of the Republicans and give Florida's four electoral votes to Tilden. The Republicans knew that; the day after the election, Zach Chandler had wired the chairman of Florida's Republican Party, HAYES DEFEATED WITHOUT FLORIDA. The Florida man replied, IF FLORIDA IS IMPORTANT, AUTHORIZE ME TO DRAW ON YOU FOR $2000. That was simply an advance against the sums that would be needed to insure the state for Hayes. By nightfall, William Chandler was rushing toward Florida on an express train, well supplied with Republican funds.

When he got there he found four Democratic visiting statesmen ahead of him. They had already checked over the returns and determined that Tilden had legitimately won in Florida by a narrow margin. The Republican-controlled returning board, though, had the power to throw out any returns "so irregular, false, or fraudulent that the board shall be unable to determine the true vote." In effect the law gave the returning board the right to name the winner as it pleased. On November 27 the board began to go over the returns in the presence of visiting statesmen of both parties.

Behind the scenes, frantic negotiations were taking place. Manton Marble, one of Tilden's men, wired Tilden's nephew, W. T. Pelton in New York on December 2, HAVE JUST RECEIVED A PROPOSITION TO HAND OVER AT ANY HOUR REQUIRED TILDEN DECI-

SION OF BOARD AND CERTIFICATE OF GOVERNOR FOR $200,000. In New York, Tilden's staff accepted the deal without telling the candidate. For a few days it seemed certain that the presidency had successfully been purchased by the Democrats. Then the arrangement suddenly collapsed, possibly because Tilden found out about it. No bribe was paid. The Florida Democrats had to fall back on the simple argument that their man had won a majority of state's votes.

That argument was not good enough. The returning board, having no reason now to go against normal party loyalties, did the expected. By a vote of 2–1, it threw out so many Democratic ballots that the Tilden majority of 93 was converted into a Hayes majority of 924. On December 5, the returning board finished its work and declared that the electors pledged to Hayes had won. The next day, they met and cast their four electoral votes for the Republican candidate. Francis Barlow of New York, one of the Republican visiting statesmen, was so appalled by this maneuver that he bluntly told his fellow Republicans that Tilden deserved Florida's votes. All he accomplished was the end of his own political career.

The tale of the Florida electoral votes had several more twists. The Democratic electors also met and sent in ballots, while protesting the illegality of the Hayes vote. Florida Democrats then went to court to declare the actions of the returning board void. On December 23, the Florida Supreme Court ruled that the returning board had acted improperly, both in the presidential contest and in the contest for governor. A recount in the gubernatorial race was ordered. In November the Republican candidate, Stearns, had been named the winner over the Democrat, Drew. But the recount showed that Drew had been elected governor. He took office in January 2, 1877, and promptly appointed a new returning board made up entirely of Democrats.

The Florida legislature, now redeemed and dominated by Democrats, passed an act directing that the new returning board go over the presidential returns. The board did so, and on January 19 announced that Tilden had carried Florida by 87 votes. The Democratic electors met at once, voted a second time for Tilden, and Governor Drew signed the certificate. It was forwarded to Washington. Congress now had *three* sets of electoral votes from Florida: a set for Hayes dated December 6 and signed by Governor Stearns, a set for Tilden dated December 6 and signed by no governor, and a set for Tilden dated January 19 and signed by Governor Drew.

If the Florida outcome was confusing, the Louisiana vote was pure chaos. The returning board there consisted of four members, all Republican; the fifth member, a Democrat, had resigned before the election and his place had not been filled. One of the Republicans was a saloonkeeper, another an undertaker. The head of the board, a carpetbagger by the name of J. M. Wells, had been called "a political trickster and a dishonest man" in 1867 when General Sherman had had to remove him as Governor of Louisiana. This disreputable board had wide powers of inquiry; it could throw out the vote in any parish (as Louisiana counties are called) where it believed force or fraud had affected the result.

The Democrats had waged a clever campaign on Election Day. In districts where they were sure to win, they saw to it that the voting was orderly and proper. But in areas of heavy Negro population, where the Republicans were likely to collect many votes, the Democrats employed terrorism so that they could later demand that the returning board throw the votes out. The Republicans countered by rigging the voting so that many Negroes voted more than once. In the turmoil, some days passed before the ballots could be counted. When the totals finally emerged, they showed that the eight Tilden electors had beaten the eight Hayes electors by margins ranging from 6,300 to 9,000 votes. It was up to the corrupt returning board to save the state for Hayes.

The Republican visiting statesmen who descended on New Orleans entered into dealings with the carpetbagger officials to insure a Hayes victory. Some of the correspondence was later made public, such as a letter to Senator John Sherman from two Louisiana Republicans dated November 20:

"We have carefully considered the arguments advanced by you in your interview. Your assurance that we shall be taken care of is scarcely specific enough. In case we pursue the course suggested by you, we would have to leave the state. Will you therefore state in writing who we shall look to for the fulfillment of these promises?"

Evidently Sherman had dangled some kind of offer before these two men if they would influence the Louisiana returning board to swing the election to Hayes. His reply, though, was a cagey one, avoiding any specific terms:

"Neither Mr. Hayes, myself, the gentlemen who accompany me or the country at large can ever forget the obligation under which you will have placed us, should you stand firm in the position you have taken. From a long and intimate acquaintance with Gov. Hayes I am justified in assuming responsibility for promises made and will guarantee that you shall be provided for. . . ."

Actually, Sherman was far more honorable a man than this exchange of letters indicates. He knew that the ballots showed the Tilden electors ahead in Louisiana; but he believed that the Democrats had achieved this only through the "bulldozing," or intimidation, of thousands of Negro voters, and that in a clean election Hayes would have won by a large margin. In a letter to Hayes on November 23, Sherman wrote:

"We are now collecting the testimony as to the bulldozed parishes. It seems more like the history of hell than of civilized and

Christian communities. The means adopted are almost incredible, but were fearfully effective upon an ignorant and superstitious people. That you would have received at a fair election a large majority in Louisiana, no honest man can question; that you did not receive a majority is equally clear. But that intimidation of the very kind and nature provided against by the Louisiana law did enter into and control the election . . . I believe as firmly as that I write this." Sherman spoke of the Louisiana returning board rather too generously as "firm, judicious, and, as far as I can judge, thoroughly honest and conscientious."

These words were intended to reassure the uneasy Hayes that nothing illegal was taking place on his behalf in Louisiana. Nevertheless, it is impossible to say what the real outcome of a completely fair election there would have been. Negroes outnumbered whites in Louisiana at that time by about 10,000. In a free election, with all these Negroes permitted to vote, nearly all would have supported the Republicans, and Hayes would have won. On the other hand, most of these former slaves were illiterate and barely knew what the election was all about. They voted only because Republican whites took them to the polls and told them which candidate to support. In a completely free election, thousands of Negroes would probably have neglected to vote altogether through sheer indifference—giving the election to Tilden. It is hard to see which is more fraudulent: keeping Negroes from voting by threats of violence, or forcing them to vote according to the wishes of political bosses. In any event, what should have mattered in Louisiana was the actual votes in the ballot boxes—and these clearly favored Tilden.

The Democrats among the visiting statesmen knew from the start that the Republicans were trying to buy Louisiana's electoral votes. Henry Watterson wired Tilden, WELL-ORGANIZED PLAN SUPPORTED BY TROOPS TO CHEAT US IN COUNT OF VOTES. OUR

MAJORITY 7750. From another aide came the gloomy word, I AM CONVINCED THEY WILL COUNT YOU OUT. Tilden took no action.

Evidently dissatisfied by the price offered by the Republicans, the returning board went shopping among the Democrats for bribes. J. M. Wells, the board's head, sent a man to Hewitt in New York City to guarantee a Democratic victory for $1,000,000. When Hewitt refused, Wells cut the price to $200,000. Evidently this offer was taken seriously for a while by Tilden's nephew, W. T. Pelton, who was less scrupulous about bribery than his uncle. Another man offered the state's vote to Henry Watterson for $250,000. Fifteen years later, Abram Hewitt said, "Louisiana has determined the result of a presidential election. The vote . . . was offered to me for money, and I declined to buy it. But the vote of that state was sold for money."

Encouraged by Republican visiting statesmen, and taking heart from the presence of regiments of Federal soldiers in New Orleans, the returning board started throwing out votes on November 20. The task proved a difficult one, since it could reject ballots only in parishes where there had been force or fraud, and most of the obvious force or fraud had taken place in districts that had voted for Hayes. It was necessary to make sure that for each Republican vote thrown out, five or six Democratic votes were disqualified.

These complex labors took twelve days. When all was done, the returning board had invalidated about 13,250 Democratic votes and 2,040 Republican votes. The net effect was to wipe out the Tilden majority and make the eight Hayes electors the winners by amounts ranging from 4,626 to 4,712 votes. It was a brazen steal, as even the Republicans admitted. Not long afterward, William E. Chandler calmly explained: "In Louisiana there had been thrown into the ballot box over 7,000 more votes for the Tilden than for the Hayes electors, and to make him President it became necessary for the returning board, acting under peculiar local laws, to throw out more than 7,000 Tilden votes on account of alleged murder, riot, and intimidation in preventing a fair and free election in certain parishes. To perform this extraordinary, even if justifiable work . . . required men of undaunted courage."

On December 6, the returning board proclaimed the Republican electors the winners, and Governor William P. Kellogg gave them certificates of election. They met and voted for Hayes on the same day. However, Louisiana had had two governments since the 1872 election. Kellogg, the Republican, had been put into office by Federal troops; but his Democratic opponent, John McEnery, had claimed victory and was recognized by the diehard whites as the true governor. McEnery's attempt to seize the office by force in 1874 had been foiled by the soldiers at the orders of President Grant, and since then not much had been heard from him. Now he reappeared to challenge the right of Kellogg to certify the electors. McEnery declared that the decision of the returning board had been improper and that the Tilden electors were the ones entitled to cast the state's presidential vote. He gave them certificates of his own; they went through the motions of voting for Tilden and Hendricks, and sent their votes to Washington to be counted with the others.

By nightfall on December 6, 1876, the electors in all 38 states had finished their work—and the nation still had no idea who would be the next President. Four states—South Carolina, Florida, Louisiana, and Oregon—had sent in double or triple sets of electoral votes. With 185 votes needed for victory, Tilden was agreed to have clearly won 184, and Hayes 163. Both sides were claiming the 22 disputed electoral votes. To impartial observers it was fairly apparent that Hayes had won in Oregon and South Carolina, and that Tilden had won in Florida and Louisiana. If so, Tilden had 196 electoral votes and the presidency. Even if he got just one of the 22 disputed votes, he would be the winner. Hayes, however, needed to gain all 22 votes to have the necessary 185.

It still seemed likely that Tilden would emerge from the crisis as President. Everything depended, though, on one question: Who was going to decide which set of electoral votes to accept?

8

───═»《◉》«═───

Who Counts the Votes?

Rarely in American history has the Constitution of the United States been studied by as many citizens as it was early in December 1876. The revered document was subjected to searching analysis in the hope that it would yield some solution to the national dilemma. But the Constitution, alas, did not provide enough guidance.

The original provisions for choosing a President had been part of Article II. In practice, those provisions had not worked out well, since they permitted an outcome in which the President could be of one party and the Vice-President of another, and so the Constitution had been amended in 1804. This amendment, the twelfth, was the law of the land at the time of the Hayes-Tilden election. It declared:

"The Electors shall meet in their respective states, and vote by ballot for President and Vice-President, one of whom, at least, shall not be an inhabitant of the same state with themselves; they shall name in their ballots the person voted for as President, and in distinct ballots the person voted for as Vice President, and they shall make distinct lists of all persons voted for as President, and of all persons voted for as Vice-President, and of the number of votes for each, which lists they shall sign and certify, and transmit sealed to the seat of the government of the United States, directed to the President of the Senate;—The President of the Senate shall, in the presence of the Senate and House of Representatives, open all the certificates and the votes shall then be counted;—The person having the greatest number of votes for President, shall be the President, if such number be a majority of the whole number of Electors appointed. . . ."

That seemed clear enough, except at a close look. It said, "The President of the Senate shall . . . open all the certificates and the votes shall then be counted." Counted by whom? And what did "counting" mean? Did the one who counted the votes have the right to decide which votes were valid and which were not? Or was he simply supposed to arrive at a total, without presuming to evaluate the worth of any of the votes?

Many Republicans argued that the Constitution directed the President of the Senate to count the votes. This was by no means necessarily true, since the Constitution's wording was vague, saying merely "the votes shall then be counted." The Republicans went on further to claim that the President of the Senate had the right to decide which votes should be counted and which should be thrown out. That year the President of the Senate was a Republican, Senator Thomas W. Ferry of Michigan. Given the power, he would certainly throw out all the disputed Tilden votes and declare Hayes to be President-elect.

The Democrats knew this, and the Democrats objected loudly. They asserted that the Constitution said nothing at all about allowing the President of the Senate to determine the validity of electoral votes. All he could do was count them, and he would have to set aside the returns from those states that were in doubt. With the disputed votes rejected entirely, neither candidate would have a majority of the electoral tally. The Constitution provided quite specifically for the steps to be taken if no candidate achieved a majority in the Electoral College:

"From the persons having the highest numbers not exceeding three on the list of those voted for as President, the House of

Representatives shall choose immediately, by ballot, the President. But in choosing the President, the votes shall be taken by states, the representation from each State having one vote; a quorum for this purpose shall consist of a member or members from two-thirds of the states, and a majority of all the states shall be necessary to a choice."

Twice in the past, Presidential elections had actually been decided this way in the House of Representatives. The 1800 election resulted in a tie between Thomas Jefferson and Aaron Burr, each with 73 electoral votes. After a long deadlock, the House elected Jefferson President. In 1824, with 131 electoral votes needed for a winning majority, Andrew Jackson had received 99, John Quincy Adams 84, William Crawford 41, and Henry Clay 37. The election was forced into the House of Representatives, where Adams, though he had run second in the national voting, was named President.

In 1876 the House of Representatives had a Democratic majority. If the election went to the House, Tilden would be chosen. Naturally, the Republicans refused to agree to any such arrangement.

It was a deadlock. The Republican Senate and the Democratic House each claimed the right to decide the election. A month had passed since Election Day, and no one yet knew who would become President when Grant's term expired on March 4. Suppose no President had been chosen then? Would Grant remain in the White House? Would the President of the Senate be entitled to declare himself President of the United States, as some suggested? Would the supporters of Hayes or Tilden try to seize power by force? It was a dizzying, terrifying moment for the nation. Moderate men everywhere called for some sort of compromise that would settle the dispute in time.

The trouble was that in any compromise, one man would have

to lose the election, and neither side was willing to agree to a solution that seemed unfavorable. Thus a suggestion that the members of the House and Senate, voting together, pick the winner was ignored; there were more Democrats than Republicans in the two legislative bodies combined, and Tilden would be certain to win. Similarly, the idea of letting the Supreme Court decide the election was rejected: the Supreme Court was made up mostly of Republicans, who of course could be expected to back Hayes.

It did not do any good to review previous instances of double election returns, for circumstances were different now. In 1865 a problem had arisen over the electoral votes of Louisiana and Tennessee, two Confederate states that had been readmitted to the Union. These states had voted for the Democratic presidential candidate. Both houses of Congress were then controlled by Republicans, and they passed what was termed the Twenty-second Joint Rule, which provided that the two houses could decide individually whether a state's electoral vote was valid. If either house objected, that state's vote would not be counted. By this means, the electoral votes of Louisiana and Tennessee were rejected in 1865.

The Twenty-second Joint Rule was still in effect in 1873 when the confusions of Reconstruction produced dubious electoral returns from Louisiana, Arkansas, and Georgia. The rule was invoked and the Louisiana and Arkansas votes were thrown out, along with three of Georgia's votes. Neither in 1865 nor in 1873 did these maneuvers have any effect on the outcome of the election.

But in the Congressional elections in 1874 the Democrats gained control of the House of Representatives. The Republicans in the Senate realized that under the Twenty-second Joint Rule, the Democrats would have veto power over the electoral votes of the next presidential election. If the Democrats objected to a state's vote, that vote would be thrown out, and there was nothing to stop the Democrats in Congress from throwing out so many votes that the election would be forced into the House of Representatives, which they controlled. So in January of 1876 the Senate scrapped the Twenty-second Joint Rule. If it had been in effect, the House would have rejected the disputed electoral votes and Tilden would have been elected. Without it, there were no rules to guide Congress.

Tension was rising; the country was drifting toward war. The attitudes of the two candidates at this critical moment were quite different. Hayes had overcome his qualms about the election, after some early embarrassment. Privately he still suspected that Tilden had really been elected, but he had allowed his friends to convince him that but for Democratic fraud he would have been the winner, and so it was all right for him to claim victory. On December 6, after the electors had voted, Hayes wrote, "I am overwhelmed with callers congratulating me on the results declared in Florida and Louisiana. I have no doubt that we are justly and legally entitled to the presidency. My conversations with Sherman, Garfield . . . and others settled the question in my mind as to Louisiana."

Tilden made no such claims. He preferred a policy of watchful waiting, allowing the crisis to settle itself according to the just workings of the law. His high regard for the Constitution had led him to reject all offers to sell him votes, when by purchasing only one vote he could be sure of the presidency. Now, that same regard kept him silent and inactive. He felt he had won, but would not say it.

This infuriated his friends. Abram Hewitt prepared a speech calling upon the citizens "to assemble . . . to protest against the frauds . . . and to express their determination that the people should not be robbed of their choice for President." Tilden re-

fused to let him deliver it, saying that it was an incentive to violence, and Hewitt reluctantly abandoned the idea. Other
Democrats urged Tilden to make a public appeal for justice.
Henry Watterson was unhappy over "the tense quietude on our
side." A Democrat coming out of a meeting at Tilden's Manhattan home said in despair, "Oh, Tilden won't do anything; he's
cold as a damn clam."

Though Tilden was silent, his supporters made their voices
heard. Hot-headed orators called for war if the Republicans succeeded in stealing the election. A mass meeting in Indianapolis
was told that "millions of men" would "offer their lives for the
sacredness of the ballot. . . . Whosoever hath a sword, let him gird
it on." The slogan, "Tilden or blood!" was heard in many places.
"Tilden-Hendricks Minute Men" clubs, dedicated to a military
defense of the Democratic victory, sprang up in eleven states.
Henry Watterson called for 100,000 citizens to march on Washington to seek justice for Tilden, and the newspaper editor Joseph
Pulitzer added that the 100,000 should "come fully armed and
ready for business." A "People's Indignation Convention" was
held in Columbus, Ohio, right under Governor Hayes' nose, and
cheered a speaker who roared, "Resistance to tyranny is obedi-
ence to law!" The convention adopted a resolution declaring that
any attempt to settle the election by the decision of the President
of the Senate should be "resisted by the people to the last extremity, even should that extremity be an appeal to arms."

Most of these wild threats came from northern Democrats. The
Democrats in the South were not nearly so excited about the possibility that Tilden would be "counted out." Certainly few Southerners were interested in going to war to make Tilden President.
The South had been devastated terribly in the Civil War, its wealth
virtually wiped out. More than a billion dollars' worth of slave
property had been lost; invading Union armies had set whole

cities ablaze; heavy taxes imposed by carpetbagger overlords had turned the white aristocracy of the South into paupers. The Panic of 1873 had fallen with particular harshness on the South, which was not yet recovered from the catastrophic losses of the war. The mood there was one of despair; the South had neither the strength nor the resources to fight a new war now merely for the sake of keeping Hayes out of the White House.

During the debates in Congress in December, southern Democrats worked patiently toward a compromise and tried to soothe the angry Northerners who talked of fighting. Senator David M. Key of Tennessee said the nation was "on the brink of danger" and urged his colleagues to "be calm, considerate, and, as far as possible, dispassionate." He called for Tilden's election but said he would have nothing to do with "violent measures." When northern Democrats demanded military action, Southerners told firsthand tales of the sufferings of war—something that the North, untouched during the war, knew little about. Governor Augustus H. Garland of Arkansas, a prominent Democrat, said, "We all conclude we want no war, no trouble, and deprecate every appearance of placing the South in any hostile attitude toward the federal government."

These words of peace from the South encouraged the backers of Hayes. They began to see the possibilities of a compromise where, to avoid war, the South would agree to letting Hayes become President. In return, President Hayes would put an end to carpetbagger rule and would take other steps to rebuild the shattered southern economy. As early as December 1, this idea had occurred to Hayes himself. An important southern newspaper editor, Colonel W. H. Roberts of the New Orleans *Times,* paid a call on Hayes at Columbus. Roberts sounded Hayes out on his views about the South, and Hayes told him "that carpetbag governments had not been successful; that the complaints of the southern people were just in this matter; that he should require absolute justice and fair play to the Negro, but that he was convinced this could be got best and most surely by trusting the honorable and influential southern whites."

Roberts replied that such a policy would attract southern support for Hayes. "You will be President," the editor said, according to Hayes' diary. "We will not make trouble. We want peace."

On December 12, Congressman James A. Garfield of Ohio sent an account of doings in Washington to Hayes which also stressed the chances of a deal with the South. Garfield wrote of the "ugly" behavior of "the more violent Democratic leaders" who were "trying to create as much sensation and popular clamor as possible," but said, "The Democratic businessmen of the country are more anxious for quiet than for Tilden; and the leading southern Democrats in Congress . . . are saying that they have seen war enough, and don't care to follow the lead of their northern associates." Garfield wondered if Hayes could subtly inform these Southerners, "who are dissatisfied with Tilden and his violent men," that "the South is going to be treated with kind consideration by you." Another Republican said the same thing: "Many of the Southern men care nothing for Tilden and distrust the Northern democrats." The seeds of compromise had been planted.

Meanwhile Congress was struggling to break its deadlock and set up machinery to decide the election. On December 7, Representative George W. McCrary of Iowa, a Republican, introduced a bill to appoint a committee of five Republicans and five Democrats that would seek a solution. President Grant, who favored a compromise, asked Abram Hewitt if he would agree to this plan. Hewitt said he would. After some debate, the size of the committee was increased to fourteen members, and it was given the power of preparing a bill that would remove all doubts about the election. On December 22, the President of the Senate named four Republican Senators and three Democrats to this Committee on Electoral Count. The Speaker of the House named four Democratic Representatives and three Republicans. A Democrat, Representative Henry B. Payne of Ohio, was chosen as chairman. Among the other members were Senator Oliver Morton of Indiana, Senator Roscoe Conkling of New York, Hewitt, and McCrary, the originator of the committee idea.

The Christmas holidays brought an end to political activity before the committee had a chance to meet. During the holidays both sides considered the next steps. What kind of compromise would emerge from the committee sessions?

The two candidates themselves disliked the thought of compromise. Hayes had now been thoroughly convinced by John Sherman that he had been fairly elected, and he saw no reason why he should get involved in dealings that might deprive him of the presidency. "I fully expect to be inaugurated," he told his friends.

Tilden, too, regarded himself as President-elect, and feared that a negotiated settlement would take from him what was rightfully his. The Republicans, using the power of the President, the Senate, and the Army, were in such a strong position that they could very well dominate any negotiations. To make things worse, Tilden had begun to hear stories that certain southern Democrats were planning to betray him in return for political favors from Hayes. "The friends of Hayes are certainly bidding high in that direction," said A. M. Gibson, a Washington newspaperman, "and I *know* that their propositions are being entertained—listened to, considered." Gibson asked a friend, Charles A. Dana of the New York *Sun,* to "give Tilden a hint." Dana forwarded Gibson's letter to Tilden on December 15, and for once Tilden moved swiftly, for he saw that everything was in jeopardy. He notified Hewitt in Washington, and the next day Hewitt called a meeting of southern Democrats to find out what was going on. He warned the Southerners not to strike any deals with the Hayes group, but he had little effect on their plans.

Tilden spent most of December preparing a book on the history of presidential elections, designed to help Congress understand the intricacies of the situation. His staff assembled an account of all official records, debates, rules, and laws on the counting of electoral votes from the time of George Washington onward, and from this Tilden compiled a work called *The Presidential Counts* that was placed on the desk of every member of Congress before the end of the month. The study showed that the Constitution was unclear on the matter of the electoral vote, and that Congress itself had the privilege of choosing the rules by which the votes were to be counted.

Tilden's book made three important points:

(1) That the two houses of Congress had the power to decide how to count the votes, and had exercised that power since the beginning of the government.

(2) That the President of the Senate merely opened the votes and presented them to Congress for counting, and had never in the past been allowed to decide whether a state's votes were valid.

(3) That the Senate and House had the power to rule on the legality of votes, and that in case of doubt they could "go behind the vote," that is, investigate the details of the election.

He supported these arguments with a formidable array of sources and references. The work was so impressive that it convinced even the Republicans that it would be improper to allow the President of the Senate to rule on the validity of votes. They had to admit the dangers of letting one man alone decide which votes counted. Tilden used his historical material as the basis for a proposal for settling the dispute. The Twenty-second Joint Rule, he said, should be revived, so that no electoral votes would be accepted if either house of Congress objected to them. The election should be decided by the votes of the House and Senate. If the two houses rejected so many electoral votes that neither candidate had a majority, the House of Representatives should choose the President as decreed by the Constitution.

Aside from knocking down the proposal that the President of the Senate be empowered to evaluate the votes, Tilden's book accomplished little. The Republicans would never accept his plan of a joint House-Senate vote. There were 57 more Democrats than Republicans in the two houses combined, and they would make Tilden President. The result would be the same if the election somehow were thrown into the House, where the Democrats had a majority of 74. So the stalemate dragged on into the new year.

The fourteen-man Committee on Electoral Count met at the beginning of January and considered suggestions for ending the crisis. Meanwhile, other Congressional committees were investigating the doubtful elections. Three groups of Representatives were at work in South Carolina, Louisiana, and Florida. The Senate had sent delegations to those three states and Georgia, Alabama, Mississippi, and Oregon as well. Some 13,000 pages of testimony were compiled, with many revealing and shocking accounts of illegalities. But the result of all this toil was predictable and useless. The Democratic-controlled House committees said that the votes of the disputed states ought to go to Tilden. The Republican-controlled Senate committees said the votes should go to Hayes.

The divided nation, caught in the turmoil of political feuding, cried out for a solution. Many ideas were offered: that both candidates withdraw so that a new election could be held; that a special commission be appointed to pick a winner; that Hayes and Tilden each appoint one arbiter who together would choose a third.

Nearly everything was suggested except a duel between Hayes and Tilden for the presidency.

One plan in particular gradually evolved out of the various suggestions. This was the appointment by Congress of an impartial Electoral Commission which would have the power to rule on the disputed votes. Several times in the past such an idea had been put forth, without success. In 1800 a law had been offered setting up an electoral council consisting of six Senators, six Representatives, and the Chief Justice of the Supreme Court, but it did not pass. In 1875, Oliver Morton had offered a similar bill, as though he foresaw the crisis of 1876. This, too, failed.

As early as November, John Sherman and some other Republicans evidently had discussed such a plan as a means of getting Hayes into the White House. President Grant had favored it. So did Abram Hewitt, when he heard of it, since he believed a truly impartial commission would surely elect Tilden. Tilden, however, was firmly against the idea. He insisted that a commission might rob him of the presidency, and that it was wrong to take the risk; let the House of Representatives settle the dispute, Tilden said.

Hewitt and other Democrats tried to persuade Tilden to agree to the formation of the Electoral Commission. They pointed out that the Republicans would never permit the House to choose the President. Besides, Tilden's reliance on the Constitution was in error, they argued. The Constitution allows the House to elect a President only when no candidate gets a majority of the electoral vote; but first the disputed votes would have to be rejected, and in the present situation there was no way either to reject or accept the multiple sets of returns. Only through the creation of a special body—the Electoral Commission—could this be done.

Slowly Tilden's objections weakened. On January 10, the seven House of Representatives members of the Committee on Electoral Count met to consider a plan proposed by President

Grant, under which Supreme Court Chief Justice Morrison R. Waite and four Associate Justices chosen by lot would comprise the Electoral Commission. Hewitt thought it might work, and two days later the seven Senators of the committee were approached for their views.

Meetings of the full committee went on for five days. At the first joint session, one Senator proposed a thirteen-man Electoral Commission, consisting of nine members of Congress and four Justices of the Supreme Court. The nine Congressmen were to be chosen by having each house name five, then dropping one by lot. The next day, the plan was amended so that five Justices would be proposed and one of these, too, be eliminated by lot. This led to a further modification. Under the new arrangement, the House and Senate would select five commissioners apiece. The names of six Supreme Court Justices would be placed into a hat and one drawn out. He would be eliminated; the other five Justices would join the ten Senators and Representatives on the fifteen-man Electoral Commission. The committee members, Democrats and Republicans, shook hands on this. Then Hewitt headed for New York to explain the agreement to Tilden.

Tilden's mood was frosty. He did not like the scheme, and was especially angered when Hewitt told him that the Democratic members of the committee "were already absolutely committed to this bill." The implication was that they were pushing the plan through, whether Tilden liked it or not, to end the long period of national confusion.

"Is it not rather late, then, to consult me?" Tilden asked.

"They do not consult you," Hewitt replied. "They are public men and have their own duties and responsibilities. I consult you."

They went over the bill together. Tilden still did not care for the whole idea of an Electoral Commission. He regarded it as a hasty plan which might do great mischief and thwart the voters who had elected him President. However, he realized that some sort of compromise had to be reached before March 4, so he decided to express neither approval nor disapproval of the proposal. He would leave the responsibility for ending the deadlock entirely to Hewitt and the other committee members. On one point, though, he was adamant. If an Electoral Commission did come into being despite his wishes, he would not approve of the elimination of one Justice by lot. "I may lose the presidency," he declared, "but I will not raffle for it." The members of the Commission must be chosen openly and with the full awareness of both sides.

Hewitt returned to Washington to conclude the arrangements. Many Democrats thereafter thought that Tilden had given his blessing to the Electoral Commission, but he had not. He continued to feel that such a tribunal was unnecessary, and that the House of Representatives alone could choose the new President. Yet he would not take the responsibility of torpedoing the compromise plan. He remained aloof, letting matters take their course, once more.

News of the proposal now had leaked out to the newspapers and the general public. No one liked it much. The Democrats thought it would give the election to Hayes, and the Republicans thought it would give the election to Tilden. The New York *Times* said that Hayes and Tilden might just as well cut cards for the presidency. One leading Democrat said it was wrong "that the great office of President should be raffled off like a Thanksgiving turkey." Hayes bitterly attacked the plan and claimed that the President of the Senate had the right to count the votes, after all.

But compromise was in the air. The Electoral Commission plan had one great virtue: neither side knew whom it favored. At last, there was a way out of the dilemma. The Democrats and Republicans were equally uneasy about the scheme, which meant that there was hope for an honest decision. Hayes' idea of letting the President of the Senate decide would bring an automatic Hayes victory; Tilden's plan of letting the House of Representatives decide would bring an automatic Tilden victory. But there was nothing automatic about the verdict of the Electoral Commission. On January 18, 1877, the Committee on Electoral Count presented a revised proposal to Congress. These were its main provisions:

(1) A fifteen-member Electoral Commission is to be appointed, consisting of five Senators, five Representatives, and five Justices of the Supreme Court. Four Supreme Court Justices shall be designated by Congress in the bill, and they are to choose a fifth Justice themselves from among their remaining colleagues.

(2) The Senate and the House of Representatives shall meet in joint session on the first Thursday in February to count the electoral votes. The President of the Senate shall preside; the meeting place shall be the hall of the House of Representatives.

(3) If any objection is raised to the electoral vote of a state that sent in a single return, that state's vote can be excluded only by a decision of both houses of Congress, acting separately.

(4) In cases where more than one return has been received, the returns are to be opened, read, and submitted to the Electoral Commission, which "shall proceed to consider the same" and to decide by a majority what is "provided for by the Constitution." The decision of the Electoral Commission is to be final unless overruled by both houses of Congress, acting separately.

(5) The Electoral Commission is to have the power to examine "such petition, depositions and other papers, if any, as shall, by the Constitution and now existing law, be competent and pertinent in such consideration."

Approval of this plan depended on a number of unspoken assumptions. Everyone knew that the House was going to pick three

Democrats and two Republicans, and that the Senate was going to pick three Republicans and two Democrats, for a 5–5 balance in the Congressional members of the Electoral Commission. The four Justices who would be named in the bill included two Democrats and two Republicans. The man they picked as the fifth Justice on the Commission thus would hold the deciding vote. He had to be impartial indeed, or the compromise plan would never be approved.

Luckily, there was one man on the Supreme Court who qualified as a genuine independent: David Davis of Illinois. Justice Davis had helped to found the Republican Party and had supported Lincoln, who named him to the Supreme Court in 1862. But after the war he had defended the policies of President Johnson against the harsh Radical Republicans. Davis had moved so far from his own party that in 1872 and again in 1876 he had been suggested by some as a possible Democratic candidate for the presidency. He was respectable, unprejudiced, and wise, and no one could call him either a Democrat or a Republican. Davis seemed ideal; when the rest of the Electoral Commission split 7–7 on the decisions, Davis would be the man to examine the evidence and render a fair verdict.

There was the quiet understanding, then, that the four designated Justices would pick Davis to be the fifth. Even this did not altogether satisfy the Republicans in Congress. Some of them suspected that Davis was secretly partial to Tilden. Others began to fear that Davis was so honest that he would have to rule against Hayes. For nearly a week, Congress hesitated about approving the Electoral Commission bill. The Democrats, despite Tilden's misgivings, were all for it, because they believed Davis would give them the victory. The Republicans, who had invented the idea of the Commission, now were against it for the same reason.

The man who finally broke the deadlock was Senator Roscoe

Conkling of New York. This Stalwart Republican had been caus-
ing trouble for his party throughout the crisis. As a member of
the Committee on Electoral Count, Conkling had repeatedly insisted that the President of the Senate did not have the right to
count the votes. On January 5, after conferring with John Sherman, James A. Garfield wrote in his diary, *Sherman is satisfied
that Conkling is going to break with the party on the Presidential
question.* A week later, William Chandler wrote, *The evidence is
convincing that Senator Conkling is against us. . . . He is bitter,
determined, excited, and I now think means to defeat Hayes &
Wheeler.* Conkling fought hard through the month to gain accep-
tance of the Electoral Commission bill, Justice Davis and all. He
succeeded in winning many Republican Senators over to his point
of view.

On January 25, the bill came to a vote in the Senate. The Democrats spoke eloquently in support of it. So did Conkling. Some
Republicans attacked it furiously, feeling that it meant the end
of Hayes' chances. Senator Morton called it a "contrivance for
surrender." When the roll was called, it became apparent that
Conkling had insured the bill's victory. The vote was 47 in favor,
17 against. Of the 47 Senators who voted aye, 26 were Democrats
and 21 were Republicans. The 17 nay votes came from 16 Republicans—including John Sherman, Oliver Morton, and James
Blaine, who had just become a Senator—and a single Democrat.

The Democrats congratulated themselves. They were half-way
to victory. In another few hours, the House of Representatives
would also pass the bill, and the Electoral Commission would
come into being. Justice Davis would have the deciding vote, and
he would surely cast it for Tilden. The national crisis would be
over, and on March 4 the lawfully elected President Tilden would
take the oath of office.

But at two that afternoon—before the House had voted—came

incredible, shattering news. Justice Davis had just been elected Senator from Illinois! He was resigning from the Supreme Court! He would not be eligible to serve on the Electoral Commission!

It was an amazing political miscalculation. The Illinois legislature, which had the right to elect that state's Senators, had been deadlocked for weeks. Neither the Republicans nor the Democrats had been able to elect a candidate, and five independent members of the legislature held the balance of power. These independents had been voting for Davis. Suddenly, on January 25, the Democrats in the legislature switched their votes to Davis on the fortieth ballot and elected him by a narrow majority.

Things could not have worked out better for the Republicans if they had engineered the Illinois election themselves. Now Davis was eliminated from serving on the Electoral Commission, and one of the remaining four Supreme Court Justices would get his place. *All four were Republicans.*

Who was responsible for this fantastic blunder? As early as January 13, the Chicago *Tribune* had predicted that Davis would be the next Senator from Illinois. Tilden had known this, but had said nothing about it to Hewitt. Hewitt had finally learned that Davis was being considered for the Senate seat, but had convinced himself that Davis still would serve on the Electoral Commission, since his Senate term would not begin until March 4. When he learned that Davis would refuse the Commission appointment, he was stunned. For the sake of electing a Senator, the Illinois Democrats had cost their party a President.

But it was too late to defeat the bill setting up the Electoral Commission. The Senate had already passed it; the House was about to vote, and could not turn back now. Late on the afternoon of January 25 the bill easily cleared the house by a vote of 191 to 86. The Democrats voted 160 to 17 for the Commission; the Republicans voted 31 to 69 against it. Yet the Democrats knew they were dooming Tilden, and voted this way only because they had already committed themselves too deeply to the Commission in the expectation of getting Davis as the fifteenth man. The Republicans, who only that morning had been expecting to see Hayes defeated, once again felt hopes of keeping the White House.

President Grant quickly signed the bill creating the Electoral Commission, saying that it settled "a gravely exciting question." On January 30, the House chose its five members: Representatives Henry Payne, Eppa Hunton, and Josiah Abbott (Democrats); George Hoar and James Garfield (Republicans). The Senate named George Edmunds, Frederick Frelinghuysen, and Oliver Morton (Republicans), and Allen Thurman and Thomas Bayard (Democrats). Most of these men had been on the earlier Committee on Electoral Count that had devised the Electoral Commission. The four designated Supreme Court Justices—Nathan Clifford and Stephen J. Field, Democrats, and William Strong and Samuel F. Miller, Republicans—went through the motions of offering the fifth place to Justice Davis. He declined the post on the grounds that he would soon enter the Senate. The four Justices selected Justice Joseph P. Bradley in his place. Bradley had been named to the Supreme Court by a Republican President, but many of his court decisions had gone in favor of the South and against the Radical Republicans. He had a reputation for fairness and independence of thought. Hewitt called his selection "entirely satisfactory" to the Democrats. The two Democratic Justices of the Supreme Court said it was absurd to think that Bradley would wield the mighty powers of his deciding vote for narrow political ends.

A more accurate appraisal was made by Webb Hayes, the son of the Republican candidate. On the afternoon of January 31 he wired his father: THE JUDGE, IT IS BRADLEY. IN WASHINGTON THE BETS ARE 5 TO 1 THAT THE NEXT PRESIDENT WILL BE HAYES.

9

The Electoral Commission

On February 1, 1877, the members of both branches of Congress filed into the hall of the House of Representatives to count the electoral vote. A sense of high drama prevailed. Diplomats from many countries had come to watch the United States in its moment of ordeal. The galleries of the chamber were packed with visitors, who murmured in excitement as the Representatives went to their desks. As the clock struck one, the Senators began to enter the room. Senator Thomas W. Ferry of Michigan, the President of the Senate, went to the front of the hall and took the seat normally occupied by the Speaker of the House. Samuel J. Randall of Pennsylvania, who had recently become Speaker of the House upon the death of Speaker Michael Kerr, sat beside him. Four "tellers" were appointed to keep a record of the electoral vote—two Senators, two Representatives.

Senator Ferry called the joint session to order and produced a wooden box containing the certificates of the electoral votes. They would be counted, he said, in alphabetical order. Alabama thus was first. Ferry took the sealed Alabama return from the box and handed it to the tellers, who opened it and examined it.

"Alabama casts its 10 electoral votes for Samuel J. Tilden," one teller announced.

Arkansas' 6 votes were also recorded for Tilden. California's 9 and Colorado's 3 went to Hayes. Connecticut gave its 6 votes to Tilden, and Delaware gave him 3 more. No objections had been raised to the proceedings thus far. But now it was time to count the Florida returns. A hush fell over the great hall; all eyes turned to Ferry as he drew a document from the box.

"The Chair hands the tellers a certificate from the State of Florida," Ferry said.

The tellers opened it. "Four votes for Hayes," came the report.

Now Ferry gave the tellers another certificate from Florida.

"Four votes for Tilden," a teller declared.

And there was a third Florida certificate! This, too, was opened and carefully studied by the tellers, who finally announced, "Four votes for Tilden."

Senator Ferry looked around. "Are there any objections to the certificates from the State of Florida?"

There certainly were. It had been arranged in advance that all objections to electoral votes would be made in writing. A Democratic Congressman from New York objected to the first Florida certificate, and his objection was read. Then Republican Congressmen from California and Iowa filed objections to the two sets of votes in favor of Tilden.

"Are there any further objections?" Ferry asked.

There were none. He ruled that the dispute be sent to the Electoral Commission for a decision, and the session was adjourned.

The Electoral Commission met the next day, February 2, to deal with the Florida returns. Both the Republicans and Democrats sent staffs of brilliant lawyers to argue the case before the Commission. There were two main problems to decide. First, was it proper for the Commission to "go behind" the returns to find out what had really happened in Florida? Second, which of the three certificates should be counted if the Commission did not go behind the returns?

Only one of the Florida certificates fulfilled all the legal requirements: the one for Hayes. It had been filed on December 6,

1876, the day on which, by Federal law, the electors had been required to cast their ballots, and it had been signed by M. L. Stearns, the Governor of Florida as of that day. The second certificate was also dated December 6; it had been filed by the Democratic electors, who had refused to accept the corrupt ruling of the Florida returning board. But this certificate lacked a gubernatorial signature; it was signed by the Attorney-General of Florida, a Democrat.

The third certificate was dated January 19. It, too, was for Tilden, and was signed by the new Democratic governor, G. F. Drew. Under the law, it had been filed more than a month too late; but Governor Drew had not taken office in time to prevent the Republican electors from getting a signed certificate on December 6. He claimed that the work of the Republican returning board had been improper, requiring a late certificate to carry the real Florida vote.

A Democratic lawyer, David Dudley Field, was the first to speak before the Commission. Field said that the voters of Florida had chosen Tilden, but that through "jugglery" a false certificate, signed by a defeated governor, had been sent to Washington by the Republican electors. He called upon the Commission to go behind the first Florida certificate to expose the fraud committed by the state's former returning board.

For the Republicans, J. A. Kasson argued that it would violate the rights of the state of Florida if the Commission were to go behind the returns. Here, he said, is a certificate of election, dated on the proper day and signed by the lawful Governor of Florida. It favored Hayes. By what right could the Commission discard this certificate and accept the certificates of the Democratic electors? One of those certificates was signed by an officer who did not have the legal right to do so; the other one had been filed a month and a half too late. The Republican argument was based strictly on "the face of the returns." Anything that had happened between November 7 and December 6—such as a fraudulent overturning of the Florida vote by the returning board—was now a closed chapter. The Commission, said the Republicans, should not go behind the returns to find out what had taken place in that period. It should consider only the certificates filed by the electors—of which, on that basis, the Republican certificate was the only valid one.

The discussion went on for several days, and the Electoral Commission said it would announce its decision on Thursday, February 8. Everything turned on what Associate Justice Joseph P. Bradley would do. Obviously the seven Democrats on the Commission would vote for going behind the returns, and the seven Republicans from Congress would vote to accept the Hayes certificate on its face. The lone Supreme Court Justice, Bradley, would control the outcome.

On Wednesday night Bradley wrestled with his decision. A friend of his, John G. Stevens, visited him and read an opinion Bradley had written. About midnight, Stevens returned to the house of Abram Hewitt, where he was a guest, and said that he had just seen Bradley's opinion "in favor of counting the vote of the Democratic electors of the State of Florida." Hewitt was delighted. Tilden needed only one of Florida's four electoral votes and the presidency was his. In the morning, an optimistic Hewitt went to the room where the Electoral Commission was meeting, expecting to hear good news.

The anticipated 7–7 tie developed, and Justice Bradley began to read his opinion. He seemed to be casting his deciding vote in favor of Tilden, but there was a sudden change of tone in the final paragraphs, and Bradley ended by declaring that he did not feel the Commission could go behind the returns. His vote made it 8–7 against examining the details of what had happened in Florida.

Hewitt was astounded. What had gone wrong? Was it possible that Bradley had changed his opinion "between midnight and sunrise," he asked?

Harsh accusations filled the air. Charges were made that certain railroad magnates had come to Bradley late Wednesday night and bribed him to favor Hayes. Tilden remarked to a friend that a mysterious third party had offered to sell *him* Bradley's vote for $200,000, the same price for which that individual had earlier promised to sell him the Florida returning board. "That seems to be the standard figure," Tilden commented. The New York *Sun* called Bradley the tool of a conspiracy of rich Republicans who were buying the presidency for Hayes. "During the whole of that night," said the *Sun,* "Judge Bradley's house in Washington was surrounded by the carriages of visitors who came to see him apparently about the decision of the Electoral Commission. . . . These visitors included leading Republicans as well as persons deeply interested in the Texas Pacific Railroad scheme."

Bradley retorted angrily, "The whole thing is a falsehood. Not a single visitor called at my house that evening. . . . I had no private discussion whatever on the subjects at issue with any persons interested on the Republican side, and but very few words with any person." But he had had at least one visitor that night—his friend John Stevens. Furthermore, Stevens had read the pro-Tilden opinion that Bradley had written. To this, Bradley replied, "Whether I wrote one opinion, or twenty, in my private examination of the subject, is of little consequence, and of no concern to anybody." He admitted that he "wrote and rewrote the arguments and considerations on both sides" of the question of going behind the Florida returns, "sometimes being inclined to one view of the subject, and sometimes to the other," before settling on his final pro-Hayes decision.

No proof has ever been produced that Bradley was approached

by Republicans late on the night of February 8. He may very well have legitimately changed his mind by himself before dawn. Yet a number of historians suspect that Bradley's denials do not ring true. In any case, he was subjected to threats of injury or assassination during the rest of the proceedings, and his house had to be placed under guard by the government. The verbal attacks continued: Senator Lewis V. Bogy of Missouri said on the floor of the Senate, "The name of the man who changed his vote upon that commission . . . from Tilden to Hayes, Justice Bradley, will go down to after ages covered with equal shame and disgrace. . . . Never will [his name] be pronounced without a hiss from all good men in this country." Senator Bogy was, of course, a Democrat.

Despite the furore, Bradley's vote did not change again. The Electoral Commission had voted 8–7 not to go behind the Florida returns. It was an ominous sign for Tilden. The loss of Florida was inevitable, now, and on February 9 the Commission voted— again by 8 to 7—to award Florida's four electoral votes to Hayes. The Democrats were in despair. Tilden's case was stronger in Florida than in any of the other disputed states. If the Commission had given Florida to Hayes, what hope was there for Tilden in Louisiana, South Carolina, or Oregon?

The Electoral Commission reported its findings to the joint session of the Senate and House. The procedure now was for each branch of Congress to vote separately on accepting the Commission's report. The report would be binding unless both houses voted to reject it. The House, with its Democratic majority, rejected the Commission's report; but the Republican-controlled Senate accepted it, and Hayes got Florida's votes.

Now the count resumed where it had been interrupted on February 1. Georgia gave 11 votes to Tilden, Illinois 21 to Hayes, Indiana 15 to Tilden, Iowa 11 to Hayes, Kansas 5 to Hayes, and Kentucky 12 to Tilden. Then came Louisiana, whose votes were drawn from the box on February 12. Here there were two certificates, both dated December 6. One was signed by the Republican governor, William P. Kellogg, the other by the Democrat who claimed to be governor, John McEnery. Objections were raised to both certificates, and they went to the Electoral Commission for a decision.

The case was a replay of the Florida debate. The Democratic lawyers argued skillfully that Tilden had won a majority of the popular vote in Louisiana, that the actions of the returning board were highhanded and improper, and that Kellogg did not have the right to sign the certificate, since he was not a lawfully elected governor. Beyond that, two of the Republican electors from Louisiana were ineligible as Federal officeholders, while three others held state offices.

The Republicans replied that the certificate of the Tilden electors had been signed by McEnery, who was not governor. They asserted that the decision of the returning board was final, and could not be gone behind. And they claimed that even if the Commission did go behind the returns, they would find no evidence that the Republicans were guilty of fraud. As Jonathan Sherman told the Senate at this time:

"A good deal is said about fraud, fraud, fraud—fraud and perjury, and wrong. Why, sir, if you go behind the returns in Louisiana, the case is stronger for the Republicans than upon the face of the returns. What do you find there? Crime, murder, violence, that is what you find. . . . I say now, as I said two months ago, that while there may have been some irregularities, while there may have been a non-observance of some directory laws, yet the substantial right was arrived at by the action of the returning board."

The vote of the Electoral Commission was a cut-and-dried affair. Justice Bradley voted with the other seven Republicans on every point. Were two of the Republican electors ineligible to cast ballots? No, said the Commission, 8 to 7. Did the Democrats have a majority of the Louisiana popular vote? No—8 to 7. Was the composition of the returning board improper because it included only Republicans? No—8 to 7. Would the Commission go behind the returns to hear evidence of forged and falsified returns? No—8 to 7. Did Kellogg have the right to sign the certificate? Yes—8 to 7. Was the action of the returning board in awarding the state to Hayes correct? Yes—8 to 7.

The last of the monotonous string of votes was taken on February 16. Tilden's nephew wired him:

TRIBUNAL RULED OUT ALL EVIDENCE. . . . MOST OUTRAGEOUS PROCEEDING . . . GREAT INDIGNATION MANIFESTED ON ALL SIDES. . . . IF YOU HAVE ANYTHING TO SUGGEST, SEND BY MESSENGER SATURDAY NIGHT.

Tilden remained silent. The Electoral Commission was behaving about as he had expected it to do, and he found nothing more useful to say than, "I told you so." The presidency was being stolen from him by a series of 8–7 votes; far from the scene of debate, Tilden looked with chilly distaste on what was taking place, but refused to make a public protest. The machinery for settling the electoral crisis had been set in motion against his wishes. Now that machinery was devouring him, which he had known would happen.

Others took a less passive attitude. It was obvious now that the Electoral Commission was going to go right down the line in support of Hayes, awarding all 22 of the disputed electoral votes to him and completing the theft of the election from the rightful victor. To the hotheads in the Democratic camp this looked perilously like a treasonous conspiracy. Tilden was bombarded with letters registering the outrage of his admirers. "The decision overwhelms us here with astonishment and sorrow," wrote a man from New Orleans. A letter from Maine was headed, "A Nation's Disgrace." Another Democrat declared, "I would never submit to this damnable fraud." There were suggestions that Tilden should name himself President on March 4 no matter what the Electoral Commission decided, and take the White House by force, if necessary.

The Democrats in the House of Representatives proposed a special strategy to fight the Electoral Commission: a filibuster. This is a technique whereby a group of dedicated Congressmen take the floor and drone on in an endless flood of words, preventing the transaction of normal business. Unless a vote to limit debate is passed, the filibuster can continue indefinitely. In the House, where the Democrats had a strong majority, it would be impossible to choke off the filibuster against the will of the Tilden supporters.

The point of staging a filibuster is to exhaust the opposition and force it to yield so that Congress can get on with its work. It was Saturday, February 17, when the Democrats of the House met to consider a filibuster. Only fifteen days remained before Grant's term expired, on March 4, and the new President was supposed to be sworn in. The authority of the Electoral Commission would also expire on March 4. If the Democrats could somehow keep talking about irrelevant things for the next two weeks, they would prevent the completion of the electoral count by the deadline. March 4 would arrive without a President-elect to take office. What would happen then? It was impossible to predict. There might be war. There might be two Presidents. There might be a last-minute deal giving Tilden the presidency. One thing was certain: if the work of the Electoral Commission were allowed to continue this way, Hayes would win. By a filibuster the Democrats at least could keep Tilden's hopes alive.

The Democratic meeting on February 17 was a stormy one.

Angry northern Democrats introduced resolutions condemning the Electoral Commission and urging the adoption of a filibuster "with the view of multiplying issues, and thereby defeating the inauguration of the usurper." But the southern Democrats were not inclined to go along. They denounced the filibuster resolution as "unwise, unpatriotic, and revolutionary." The Southerners insisted that the work of the Electoral Commission be allowed to proceed unhindered—even though it made Hayes the next President.

The split between the Democrats of the North and the South was now at its widest. Without the support of the Southerners, the filibuster would not succeed. After the meeting, the northern Democrats told newspapermen that "the Southern Representatives have deserted in a body, so as to make fair weather with the Republican Party."

What had happened? How had the leaders of the South allied themselves with the party of reconstruction and carpetbaggery?

The secret deal had been brewing for months. Hayes and his aides had begun courting the South just after the election, with considerable success. Several emissaries from Hayes had met with influential Southerners to make it clear that if elected, Hayes would treat the South extremely favorably. The chief figures in the negotiations were William Henry Smith of Chicago, Hayes' closest personal friend; Colonel Andrew J. Kellar, editor of the Memphis *Avalanche* and a former Confederate officer; and General Henry Van Ness Boynton, who had fought on the Union side and now was a Washington newspaperman. These three in particular hatched the plot. Kellar, as a Southerner himself, was the key man. Though an ex-Confederate, he had not been greatly in sympathy with the slaveholders; as William Smith wrote to Hayes, it was Kellar's "earnest desire to aid in building up a conservative Republican party in the South, that shall effectively destroy the color line & save the poor colored people."

The deal hinged on the fact that the new leaders of the South, the Redeemers, were basically not members of the old plantation-owning aristocracy. They were businessmen from the cities: bankers, manufacturers, railroad operators. Many of them had been Whigs before the Civil War, and had drifted into the Democratic Party only because no other party existed in the South when the Whigs collapsed. These southern businessmen had never really been at home in the southern branch of the Democratic Party, which was dominated by slaveowners. They had much more in common with the northern Republicans. What the Hayes men wished to do was to split these ex-Whigs away from the southern planters and get them to support the Republican candidate.

It was a natural alliance that cut across geographical lines. Hayes had been a Whig, and the southern railroad men, industrialists, and mine owners were old Whigs too. They thought alike on matters of importance to business. The Republicans had clearly emerged as the party of Big Business. The Democrats, although their candidate was an eastern millionaire with strong business connections, were basically a party of farmers, factory workers, small shopkeepers—and, in the South, plantation-owners.

Through Smith, Kellar, and Boynton, Hayes had to show these southern business-oriented Democrats that he could do more for them than Tilden would. What the South wanted was money—government money with which it could rebuild its war-wrecked economy. In particular the Southerners wanted government cash to construct railroads, which were essential for commercial growth. They needed government help in developing canals and harbors, in building bridges, and in putting up levees, or flood-control walls. Shattered by war, plundered by carpetbaggers, crippled by the Panic of 1873, the South could do none of these things without subsidies from the national government.

The South had certainly been shortchanged in recent years when Federal money was handed out. Between 1865 and 1873, $103,000,000 had been spent on public works projects. The entire South—the eleven ex-Confederate states plus Kentucky—had received only $9,469,000. New York alone had been granted $15,688,000. Arkansas had been given all of $49,103, which compared poorly with New Hampshire's $1,285,000. Mississippi had had $136,000, and Massachusetts $3,030,000.

This was pure politics. The Radical Republicans had been in control of Congress during those years, and they had not cared to funnel government money into the despised South. They had aided their own states instead, while bridges and levees in the South destroyed in the war remained in ruins. However, the discrimination against the South went back much further. From 1789 to 1873, the government had spent $104,705,000 on railroads, canals, and roads. Just $4,430,000 of this had gone to the South. By contrast, $83,354,000 had been paid out to help build the transcontinental Union Pacific and Central Pacific railroads, which made northern speculators rich. Lacking sufficient political strength, the South had not been able to cut its fair share of the Federal pie.

Now the South was angry, and out to get what it felt was its due. The Nashville *Banner* reviewed southern history and asked what the South had to show for itself except "a great deal of glory and mighty little plunder. A few tumble down buildings and a gigantic poverty. . . ." The Vicksburg *Herald* said, "The shower of subsidies to railroads has been something more than a slight mist, and we propose that the South shall hold her dish out to catch whatever may fall her way." The New Orleans *Times* asked,

"Would any sane man believe, if that part of the Mississippi River which is able to overflow its banks, ran through northern territory, that the Government would not long ago have taken upon itself the care of building the levees?"

When the Radical Republicans were riding high, waving the bloody shirt at every opportunity, it was impossible for the South to hope for favors from the government. In the bitter aftermath of the war, the Southerners were still treated as "rebels" and were ignored when they asked for help. But Hayes was no Radical. He had taken no part in the brutalities of Reconstruction. He offered himself now as the voice of harmony and reconciliation. When he had accepted the Republican nomination in the summer of 1876 he had promised to "wipe out the distinction between North and South." Now, in the troubled period following the election, Hayes made it quite clear what that phrase meant: he would do all in his power as President to see that the South received a fair share of Federal money.

On the other hand, the man least likely to shower cash upon the South was Samuel J. Tilden. Tilden was a Democrat and the Southerners were also Democrats, but that did not mean he intended to bestow money on them. He had campaigned on a slogan of "Retrenchment and Reform." Retrenchment meant cutting government spending, reducing subsidies, halting the drain on the Treasury, saving every possible penny. Tilden was a thrifty man in person and he meant to be a thrifty President. He believed the government had spent much too much already on public works, and wanted to leave such things as bridges and canals up to the responsibility of the individual states.

His pennypinching views were shared by many of the northern Democrats who had come to power in the House of Representatives in the 1874 election. William S. Holman of Indiana, Chairman of the House Committee on Appropriations, boasted that he had cut $25,000,000 from government expenses in 1875. "No scheme of public plunder has been successful," he said. "No 'rebel claim' has reached the Treasury, no new offices have been created, but a multitude have been abolished; no salaries have been increased, but a large number have been diminished; no new scheme of public expenditure has been inaugurated, while many have been discontinued."

The prospect of four years of a Tilden presidency was a grim one for southern businessmen hopeful of economic aid from the government. Tilden was too frugal, too parsimonious. Worse, he had been forced to take some extreme anti-southern stands in his campaign, simply to meet Republican accusations. Because he had been involved in railroad speculations in his own business career, a fear arose that Tilden would continue to aid the railroads as President. He denied this so forcefully that a Democratic paper, the Cincinnati *Enquirer,* attacked him as "a most pitiless foe of the interests of the West and South" and an "unscrupulous oppressor of the great struggling industries" of those sections. The public also believed that Tilden, as a Democrat, would surrender to the "rebels" and pay off the southern claims for war damage, as well as the Confederate war debt. This could mean payments of billions of dollars if all claims were honored. Tilden issued a public denial that he would ever under any circumstances pay either claims, debts, or compensation to any "rebel" or "disloyal person."

None of this made the South happy. So when Hayes came along offering tolerance and subsidies, the southern Democrats began seriously to consider abandoning Tilden altogether.

The South needed Hayes, and Hayes needed the South. Although it was clear by mid-February that the Electoral Commission was going to award him the presidency, it was not at all clear that the nation would let him take it. A real possibility existed that the Democrats would rebel and go to war to make Tilden President. Such a civil war would be far more terrible than the earlier one, for it would not be confined to one section of the country. On every street of every town and city, Democrat might fight against Republican, turning the United States into a gigantic battlefield from coast to coast.

Hayes could not judge Tilden's attitude. The old fox was keeping silent as the electoral count proceeded; did that mean that he was biding his time, ready to give the signal for rebellion when March 4 came? Hayes knew that if he had the support of the South, if a sizable faction of Democrats recognized him as President, civil strife could be avoided. *I would like to get support from good men of the South, late Rebels,* he wrote in his diary on February 17. *How to do it is the question. I have the best disposition towards the Southern people, Rebels and all. I could appoint a Southern Democrat in the Cabinet.*

He considered naming as his Secretary of War a famous Confederate hero, General Joseph E. Johnston. But General William T. Sherman protested that this was going a little too far for the sake of reconciliation. Hayes did choose for his Postmaster General a Southerner, Senator David M. Key of Tennessee, a Democrat whose term would expire on March 4. Key had been a Confederate officer too, but not an important one, and he had not originally favored secession in 1860. When sounded out about the job, he was surprised to learn that the Republicans were willing to put a Democrat and an ex-Confederate in the Cabinet, but he said that if the Hayes Administration should "develop a broad and liberal policy towards the people of the South, I would not hesitate to incorporate my fortunes and self with it."

The Postmaster General's position was a powerful one, since it was his responsibility to appoint thousands of postmasters all over the country. Giving the valuable job to a Democrat was a high price for Hayes to have to pay. But the same weekend that he started to plan his Cabinet, the House Democrats were talking about setting up a filibuster, and Hayes needed southern support more than ever. The Southerners held the power to break the filibuster, let the electoral count continue, and deliver the presidency to Hayes. That weekend, therefore, Hayes' representatives met with the leaders of the South and worked out most of the terms by which Hayes would buy the favor of the former Confederates.

The filibuster meeting on Saturday night, February 17, left no doubt among the northern Democrats that the deal had been made and that Tilden would be betrayed. On Monday the 19th, Congress resumed its joint session and the report of the Electoral Commission on the Louisiana case was presented. To no one's surprise, the House failed to approve the report, but the Senate accepted it, and Louisiana's eight electoral votes were counted for Hayes, amid Democratic cries of "fraud" and "conspiracy."

The counting proceeded. Maine's 7 votes went to Hayes; Maryland's 8 to Tilden; Massachusetts' 13 to Hayes. A slight objection was raised but not sustained when Michigan was reached, and finally its 11 votes were tallied for Hayes. Minnesota's 5 votes were cast for Hayes; Mississippi and Missouri gave 8 and 15 votes to Tilden; Nebraska's 3 were for Hayes, as were 3 more from Nevada. New Hampshire's 5 went to Hayes, New Jersey and New York gave 9 and 35 to Tilden. North Carolina added 10 more for the Democrats, Ohio 22 for the Republicans.

Next was Oregon—another of the disputed states. The Democrats had challenged the Oregon vote because one Republican elector held a Federal office as a postmaster, and so was constitutionally ineligible to cast an electoral vote. Objections were raised, and the Oregon certificates were sent to the Electoral Commission for a verdict. Then Congress adjourned.

That night the Democrats met again. Speaker of the House

Randall, the leader of the Congressional Democrats, revived the demand for a filibuster and bluntly accused the Southerners of making a bargain with Hayes. He warned them of the dangers of trusting the Republicans; Hayes, he said, would not make good on his promises, and once in office his policies would be of "such a character as to overwhelm any southern man in ruin." Randall suggested that the House pass a bill that would make the Secretary of State the Acting President of the United States until a new election could be held. If the House remained in recess, blocking the electoral count, the Senate would be forced to pass the bill. Then Grant's term could be allowed to run out and a closely supervised election would take place.

The pro-Hayes Southerners were shaken by this counterattack. Some were so convinced by Randall's words that they recovered their wavering loyalty and considered withdrawing from the deal. A delegation of Southerners called late on the night of February 19 at the house of Representative Charles Foster of Ohio, a Republican and one of the chief negotiators between Hayes and the southern Democrats. They told Foster that there was danger that the deal would collapse unless Hayes strongly pledged himself to aid the South. Foster consulted with Garfield and several of the other Hayes lieutenants, and they agreed that the Southerners needed to be reassured.

The next day, while the Electoral Commission was mulling over the Oregon case, Foster rose in the House of Representatives to speak: "Representing as I do the district in which Governor Hayes resides, and being a life-long acquaintance of his . . . I say that his administration will be wise, patriotic, and just." As for Hayes' treatment of the long-suffering South, Foster said, "The flag shall float over States, not provinces; over freemen, and not subjects." The Southerners received these assurances warmly; the northern Democrats denounced what they saw as a shameless attempt to split their party.

One of the would-be northern filibusterers tried to slow things down by calling for a recess until the next day. The motion was defeated, 163 to 86. Thirty southern Democrats voted against it. The *National Republican,* a party newspaper, rejoiced over this coalition of Democrats and Republicans. The Southerners, it said, at last had seen that "their true friends are not among the hypocritical riffraff Copperhead faction of the North [Democrats], but among those who were brave enough to meet them like true heroes on the battlefield." It predicted that the joining of the two forces would enable the Republicans to "march to twenty years more of usefulness, power, and beneficence."

By February 22, it seemed that the filibuster crisis was over, and Hayes once again grew confident of victory. The next day, the Electoral Commission released its decision on Oregon. By the usual vote of 8 to 7, it ruled that Postmaster Watts had been a legitimate elector after all, and awarded Oregon's three votes to Hayes. The House disagreed, the Senate did not, and the decision became final.

But something had happened that morning that threatened to interrupt Governor Hayes' smooth procession to the White House. Some fifty copies of the February 22 edition of the Columbus *Ohio State Journal* appeared on the desks of leading Democratic members of the House of Representatives. This newspaper had Republican views, and it had printed a standard bloody-shirt editorial attacking the white misdeeds in Louisiana. The only remarkable feature of this was that the editor of the paper was General James Comly, one of Hayes' closest personal friends. Presumably anything Comly printed in his newspaper represented Hayes' own thoughts.

The astounded Southerners felt that they had been betrayed.

They remembered Speaker Randall's warning only four days earlier that Hayes was really a Radical Republican whose policies would "overwhelm in ruin" the South. Now the pro-Hayes Democrats were in a panic. What if they succeeded in turning the country over to a Republican usurper, only to find in him an enemy once he was safely in the presidency? The people back home, who were loyal Democrats, had begun to find out that their Congressmen were trying to dump Tilden. They did not understand the subtleties of railroad subsidies and Federal building projects. They had voted for Tilden, and they would be furious if their party's own leaders installed Hayes instead. As a man from South Carolina wrote in the *Atlantic Monthly* just then, "The excitement in the South over the presidential contest is literally frightful. Should it be adverse to Mr. Tilden, the national House of Representatives and Mr. Tilden have it in their power to cause an explosion in the South so terrific that the outbreak of 1860–61 will be almost forgotten. The most dangerous hopes and emotions are agitating the bosom of every Southerner. At every street corner and fireside, on the steps of every store, you may hear men saying that the hour of the Republicans is striking, that they have got to submit. . . ."

The southern Democrats confronted the Hayes men with the newspaper editorial. From Ohio came the explanation that General Comly was sick, that the editorial was the work of a young assistant editor, and that Hayes knew nothing of it. Even this did not soothe the worried Southerners. After the Oregon decision was announced, filibuster talk was revived, and this time the southern faction went along with it. At a meeting of House Democrats on the afternoon of February 23, the party voted to seek a recess that would adjourn the House over the weekend. Only six working days would then remain before March 4 in which to settle the election and take care of the hundreds of other matters awaiting Congressional action.

When the motion for a recess was offered on February 24, the outcome was surprising. Many of the Southerners who had voted against a recess on February 20 now voted for one. But a great many northern Democrats, pro-filibuster just a day or two ago, switched sides the other way and voted against the recess! As a result, the filibuster measure was defeated, 158 to 112. Immediately one of the filibusterers asked for a second vote on the issue. To the amazement of all, Speaker Randall ruled the suggestion out of order. The leader of the filibuster move had turned against the filibuster himself!

This twist in the tale had come about because a few of the more responsible northern Democrats had paused to consider what the consequences of a filibuster might be. Looking beyond March 4, they saw the possibility of civil war and chaos if no President were chosen. Speaker Randall, backed by Abram Hewitt, was realistic about Tilden's chances at this point: they were nonexistent. It was a choice between Hayes and chaos, and Randall and Hewitt preferred Hayes. They were bowing to the inevitable, for the sake of peace. Four years of Hayes, said Hewitt, was better than four years of civil war.

Now it was the northern Democrats who wanted the electoral count to continue, and the Southerners who talked of filibusters. The bewildered Hayes men had difficulty comprehending the rapid shifts of beliefs. John Sherman wrote to Hayes on February 24 that "all sorts of rumors are current still." It was possible that diehard Tildenites might yet resort to "revolutionary means."

In the days immediately following the publication of the damaging editorial in the *Ohio State Journal,* a series of hurried conferences took place as the Hayes men tried to patch up their alliance with the southern Democrats. It was necessary now to work out in very specific terms the nature of what Hayes promised to do for the South and what the Southerners would do for Hayes. These meetings reached a climax on February 26, when three separate gatherings were held in Washington. At one, Representative Charles Foster of Ohio met with a Democratic Representative from Kentucky and one from Georgia. At the second, Senator John Sherman and two other Hayes backers conferred with Major E. A. Burke, the most powerful newspaper editor in Louisiana. That evening, the many strands of the allliance were drawn together in a room of Wormley's Hotel, where William H. Evarts, a lawyer serving as Republican counsel before the Electoral Commission, was staying. A number of Hayes' closest advisers represented him at the Wormley's Hotel meeting, including John Sherman and James Garfield. The Democrats were represented by Major Burke, Henry Watterson, and several others.

Each of the Republicans assured the Democrats that Hayes would look out for the interests of the South. They promised that Hayes would withdraw Federal troops from the South, ending Reconstruction at long last; that he would recognize Democrats Wade Hampton and Francis Nicholls as governors of South Carolina and Louisiana, thus redeeming those states from the carpetbaggers; and that he would "deal justly and generously with the South" on the question of Federal subsidies. For their part, the Southerners agreed to block any filibuster moves and to bring about the orderly completion of the work of the Electoral Commission. They would openly recognize Hayes as the lawfully elected President of the United States. They would not abuse their positions of restored power in their own states, but promised to respect the rights of Negroes and Republicans. They guaranteed political equality, civil rights, and equal opportunities of education for the Negroes. This was a particularly important point for Hayes, who did not want to abandon the loyal Republican-voting

Negroes of the South to white rule without some sort of assurances for their welfare.

Everything was duly agreed. The South would help make Hayes President, and Hayes would give the South back to the white Democrats. Reconstruction was dead; the carpetbaggers would be chased into hiding. When the Wormley's Hotel meeting broke up, late at night on February 26, both sides had the satisfaction of knowing that a good bargain had been struck, and that the wearying weeks of unending doubt and strain would soon be over.

10

The End of the Crisis

The day of the Wormley's Hotel meeting, February 26, South Carolina had been reached in the count of the electoral votes. Since this was one of the states that had turned in conflicting certificates, the case went to the Electoral Commission.

By now both sides were merely going through the motions. The Democrats, since they had no real claim to the South Carolina vote, did not bother to present a detailed legal position; they delivered some loud political oratory and some violent denunciations aimed at the Commission, and demanded that the South Carolina certificates for both sets of electors be thrown out. The Republican lawyers calmly defended the legality of their own certificate without further argument. The Commission voted unanimously to reject the Democratic set of electors from South Carolina. Then, by the customary 8–7 decision, it accepted the Republican electors on February 28. That evening, the House denied and the Senate affirmed the ruling, and South Carolina was added to Hayes' growing list.

The count hurried on toward the finish. Tennessee's 12 votes and the 8 of Texas went to Tilden. Late in the February 28 session, Vermont was reached. No trouble was anticipated here; but Abram Hewitt, apparently convinced that he had to do something at this point to save Tilden, produced another surprise.

Senator Ferry was presiding. As he called for the Vermont vote, Hewitt rose waving a sealed package that he said contained an alternate set of Vermont returns. The set previously delivered to Congress had favored Hayes. Hewitt now claimed that one of the Republican electors was ineligible because he was a postmaster, and that he held in his hand a valid Democratic vote for Tilden.

It was the Oregon story all over again. Tilden was still looking for the one vote that would give him a majority, and Hewitt claimed to have found it for him. Democrats and Republicans alike were bewildered. Everyone had thought the business of the electoral count was all settled. Since Hayes had been awarded the Oregon vote, he would probably get the Vermont one as well— but time was running out. Four days from now, a new presidential term was supposed to begin. Was this Vermont business one final Democratic trick to stall until the end of the present term of office?

There was a great outcry. The filibusterers took heart, seeing Hewitt once more on their side. Amid wild shouting Senator Ferry ruled that the Senate and the House would have to separate to consider the Vermont problem. The Senate unanimously voted to give Vermont to Hayes; but in the House the Democrats forced an adjournment without a decision.

The House met again the following day, March 1, to take up the question of Vermont. It was one of the stormiest sessions in the history of Congress. The crosscurrents of Democratic strategy had everyone puzzled; no one could predict anyone's position any more, and the chances of a filibuster looked good. The session began at ten in the morning before packed galleries. Speaker Randall presided, and was instantly bombarded with demands by the filibusterers for a recess. He ruled all these delaying tactics out of order. From the floor came angry yells and shrieks of outrage. One Congressman stood on top of his desk to shout abuse at the Speaker. Randall furiously banged his gavel. There was a call for a debate on the Vermont vote. Randall ruled that the debate could last not more than two hours; then the count would have to proceed. This was greeted by hisses from the filibusterers, who wanted to debate the issue, if possible, through to midnight on March 4.

With Speaker Randall cutting through the disorder to keep the session moving along, the Vermont matter was taken up. The pro-Tilden Democrats insisted that the House refuse to proceed with the count until the President of the Senate had opened the second package of Vermont votes and submitted the question to the Electoral Commission. If successful, this move would delay the completion of the count by a day or two, bringing the crisis ever closer to the March 4 deadline and the unknown calamities that lay beyond it. Speaker Randall called for a vote. The result: 116 Congressmen favored the motion, but more than 150 opposed it, and it was defeated.

The filibusterers, now an irate mob, threatened to stage a noisy demonstration. When the clamor was at its loudest, Congressman William M. Levy, a Democrat from Louisiana, took the floor. Levy had been one of the negotiators at Wormley's Hotel; he spoke now on behalf of the pro-Hayes Southerners. It was the first time that a member of this faction had called openly for the election of the Republican candidate. Levy said:

"The people of Louisiana have solemn, earnest, and I believe truthful assurances from prominent members of the Republican Party, high in the confidence of Mr. Hayes, that, in the event of his election to the presidency, he will be guided by a policy of conciliation toward the southern states, that he will not use the Federal authority or the Army to force upon those state governments not of their choice, but in the case of these states will leave their own people to settle the matter peaceably, of themselves." He urged all "who have been influenced in their action . . . by a desire to protect Louisiana and South Carolina" to join him in helping to complete the count.

The effect of his words was dramatic. Dozens of southern and border-state Congressmen deserted the violent last-ditch filibuster movements. The House voted to accept the regular return for Vermont. Only a hard core of irreconcilable Tilden men opposed the vote.

Two states remained to be counted: West Virginia and Wisconsin. West Virginia had given its 5 electoral votes to Tilden, and without complications this result was accepted. Senator Ferry asked that the Wisconsin vote be taken from the box. Wisconsin's 10 electoral votes had been cast for Hayes. Unless the Democrats could find some way to wrest at least one of these votes away, Hayes would be elected President.

It was now just past midnight. Thursday, March 1, had become history; Friday, March 2, had arrived. The Congressional session had lasted more than fourteen hours, and the end had not yet come. As the discussion of the Wisconsin vote began, Representative Joseph C. Blackburn of Kentucky, a Tilden man, rose to address the members:

"Mr. Speaker, today is Friday. Upon that day the Savior of the world suffered crucifixion between two thieves. On this Friday constitutional government, justice, honesty, fair dealing, manhood, and decency suffer crucifixion amid a number of thieves."

Blackburn was shouted down. But there came a challenge to one Wisconsin elector on the grounds that he was a government pension officer. The Senate and the House separated again to consider the matter. Quickly the Senate voted to ignore the objection. In the House, another Tilden diehard, Representative Roger Q. Mills of Texas, offered a resolution calling upon the House of Representatives to proceed to elect a President of the United States, as was its constitutional privilege when no candidate had received a majority of the electoral vote. Speaker Randall ruled the proposal out of order.

Then Randall produced a telegram he had just received from Tilden. The Democratic candidate said that he was willing to let the count be completed. The statement amounted to a concession of defeat. The House voted to let the Wisconsin tally stand as before, for Hayes.

At four in the morning on March 2, the Senate filed back into the hall of the House to bring the ritual of the count to its close. Since there were no objections now in either branch of Congress to the Wisconsin vote, it was counted for Hayes. The tellers made a final tabulation. Hayes had received all the disputed votes, for a total of 185 and a majority of one. Tilden, who had had 184 votes when the Electoral Commission was formed, had the same number now. The list of all the votes was read. Then Senator Ferry arose and said:

"Wherefore, I do declare: That Rutherford B. Hayes, of Ohio, having received a majority of the whole number of electoral votes, is duly elected President of the United States for four years, commencing on the 4th day of March, 1877. And that William A. Wheeler, of New York, having received a majority of the whole number of electoral votes, is duly elected Vice-President of the United States for four years, commencing on the 4th day of March, 1877."

The agony was over. The nation would have a new President two days hence. The most spectacular political crime in American history had been accomplished. The exhausted Congressmen uttered sighs of relief, but there was no applause. Hewitt collapsed in fatigue and was taken home by friends. As the wintry dawn broke, those who had named a President slipped into their beds, the victors too abashed to feel much satisfaction, the losers stunned and bitter.

President-elect Hayes was already on his way to Washington. On Wednesday night, February 28, the state capitol in Ohio had been the scene of a glittering reception as the people of Columbus said farewell to their governor. The next day, two private cars had been attached to a Pennsylvania Railroad train, by order of Hayes' friend, Tom Scott, the head of the railroad company. A cheering throng heard Hayes speak from the rear platform of the train on Thursday afternoon; then, accompanied by his family and a few close friends, he headed East.

He was tense and embarrassed by the events in Congress. Though he believed that he had more or less legitimately won the election, he had qualms about the road he had taken to the White House, and these qualms would remain with him for the rest of his life. This essentially decent and honorable man was uncomfortably aware that he was probably usurping the presidency. It was not an easy burden to bear. There had been threats against his life, and even one assassination attempt already. Hayes knew that he might well be killed by some pro-Tilden fanatic if he took the oath of office. More than death, though, he feared scorn—the contempt of a nation that would always regard his claim to the presidency as tainted.

On Thursday night Hayes' train reached Harrisburg, Pennsylvania. It halted there, and early Friday morning he was awakened to hear the results of the electoral count. It came as no surprise, and word of his victory only heightened Hayes' mood of uncertainty and uneasiness. He was asked about the arrangements he preferred for his inauguration, and he said he wanted the ceremony to be as simple and as modest as possible. It was customary to have a great parade followed by a night of riotous celebration, but Hayes declined this. It was as though he hoped to slip into his questionable presidency unnoticed, as inconspicuously as he could.

Out of the same modesty, Hayes refused an invitation from President Grant to stay with him in the White House. Instead Hayes arranged to be the guest of Senator John Sherman. When his train arrived in Washington on Friday morning, Hayes was met by Sherman and his more famous brother, General William T. Sherman, who took him at once to the Senator's residence. Hayes breakfasted there, then paid a call at the White House. The meeting between President Grant and President-elect Hayes was casual and faintly chilly. Grant, who had been swept into office on an immense wave of national popularity, was leaving the presidency with the sad knowledge that his eight-year administration had been one of the worst, the most corrupt, and the least efficient in the country's history. Hayes himself, a candidate of reform, had campaigned in part against the sorry record of the Grant Republicans. Yet here was the new President already stained by irregularities, and he was not even installed in his office.

Grant and Hayes drove together from the White House to the Capitol, where the President-elect met Congressmen of both parties and the members of Grant's Cabinet. Hayes received a particularly warm welcome from the southern Democrats, who felt they "owned" him after their services in making him President. Behind their cheerful cordiality lay the happy knowledge that they would soon be collecting the great debt Hayes owed them.

Public reaction to the end of the crisis started to appear on Saturday, March 3. The Washington *Union,* a newspaper founded by Tilden as the national organ of his presidential campaign, went out of business that day, printing in its final edition the declaration, "Fraud has triumphed, and triumphed through the treachery of Democrats. Honest men of irresolute nature and dull perceptions have assisted, but corruption led the way." That same day the Cincinnati *Enquirer* protested, "It is done. And fitly done in the dark. By the grace of Joe Bradley, R. B. Hayes is 'Commissioned' as President, and the monster fraud of the century is con-summated." The New York *Sun* put a black border around its pages, to show mourning for the death of democracy.

The Democrats of the House soothed their wounded pride Saturday morning by passing a resolution over Republican opposition that proclaimed that Tilden had been "duly elected President of the United States for the term of four years, commencing on the 4th Day of March, A.D., 1877." It was only a token gesture, with no force of law. Yet it could have served as the spark to ignite civil war, if Tilden had been so minded.

Many of Tilden's friends and backers were certainly so minded. Telegrams flooded into his New York City home all day, attacking the outrageous decision. From New Orleans came this message: WILL THE DEMOCRATS SEE A USURPER IN THE CHAIR OF WASHINGTON? . . . SAY, NO! NEVER!! IN TONES THAT WILL RESOUND FROM OCEAN TO OCEAN. IF YOU SAY THE WORD, 50,000 LOUISIANANS WILL TAKE UP GUNS FOR YOU. A Philadelphia man wired, COUNSEL RESISTANCE. WE DARE NOT SUBMIT TO FRAUD. From a Texas Negro came the hope that RIGHT JEHOVAH WILL SUSTAIN YOU. Tilden was advised to appeal to the Supreme Court to have the ruling of Congress overturned—which would have done no good, since the Supreme Court was made up mostly of Republicans. Several messages begged Tilden to "repair the past in the future" by running again in 1880. Charles Francis Adams, the descendent of two Presidents, sent his sympathies, and complimented Tilden on "the calm and dignified manner in which you have passed through the great trial."

The Democratic leaders in Congress—particularly Hewitt and Speaker Randall—were accused of selling Tilden out to the Republicans for the sake of avoiding a national split. "The long agony is over—a thief is President," said one writer, who blamed the outcome on Hewitt's "timid, vacillating, halting, hesitating course." Another said, "We had a first-class case, but we lost it by imperfect pleadings." Hewitt himself, who had done a great deal to defeat Tilden, was in an extremely awkward position, and he knew it. He had helped to set up the Electoral Commission in the mistaken belief that it would make Tilden President. After the David Davis blunder, Hewitt had realized that Tilden's case was lost, and he had sought to insure harmony in the land by working toward a Hayes victory. Hewitt had defeated the filibuster and had been one of the engineers of the deal between the southern Democrats and the northern Republicans—only to swing around again, to save his own face, in the last-minute fight over the Vermont certificate. Now Hewitt resigned as Chairman of the Democratic National Committee. In 1886 Hewitt revealed that he had spent most of that final weekend trying to undo the damage he had caused, and trying to create even more serious damage:

"I spent three days in forming a letter for Mr. Tilden, saying to the American people that he believed himself to be the President-elect, and that on the fourth day of March, eighteen seventy-seven, he would come to Washington to be inaugurated." Hewitt took the letter to New York and tried to get Tilden to sign it. But Tilden, who had shrugged off his defeat with a faint smile and the whispered words that it was what he had expected, wanted no part of a *coup d'état*. He refused to sign Hewitt's letter, and thus, as Hewitt wrote later, "threw the presidency away."

Hewitt's *Secret History* of the 1876 election, not published until 1937, blamed Tilden for his own defeat, saying, "The habit of Mr. Tilden's mind was to criticize and postpone, not to decide." True, Tilden had hesitated during the critical moments of the post-election dispute, and Tilden now refused to proclaim himself President as the moment of inauguration neared. But Tilden had acted out of honor and respect for the law, not out of paralysis of will. He could not seize the presidency, for it went against every principle he believed in. Even though he knew he had been unjustly deprived of victory, he acquiesced in the injustice, since Congress had formally counted him out. Tilden's real mistake had been in his choice of campaign lieutenants. He had tried to do too much himself, hiding his deepest strategies from those about him. There was never any real contact between Tilden and Hewitt, and in the end Hewitt's muddled political dealings lost the presidency for him. First Hewitt wanted peace at any price, then civil war, and as he swung from pole to pole, the canny Republican negotiators pushed Hayes to victory.

Congress wound up its business that Saturday in a flurry of late activity. There was a final maneuver of the Tildenites that showed how much trouble the diehards could still make. One bill that remained unpassed was the pay bill for the Army. Until Congress passed it, the soldiers could not receive their wages. On February 19, the Democrats in the House had tacked onto this bill an amendment specifying that Federal troops could not be used to support the claims of any of the rival state governments in the South "until the same shall have been duly recognized by Congress." That is, it would be illegal for the next President to bolster the Republican administrations in Louisiana or South Carolina against the wishes of Congress. If he violated this measure, the President would be subject to imprisonment "at hard labor for not less than five nor more than ten years."

This clause was an absurd infringement on the powers and rights of the President. The House passed it, but the Senate knocked it out of the appropriations bill. In the last hectic hours of the Congressional session on March 3, conferees from the House and Senate argued over the clause. The Republicans argued that Hayes would live up to his promise and allow Democratic administrations to take control of the remaining unredeemed southern states, but the Democrats insisted on making sure of it by writing the non-interference requirement into the appropriations bill. The deadlock continued as the clock ticked away. The Democrats would not yield. At midnight on Saturday, the Forty-fourth Congress adjourned forever, and no appropriations bill for the Army had been passed. President Hayes would have to govern with the aid of unpaid and unhappy troops until the new Congress could agree. As it turned out, the Army did not get its pay until November 30—by which time the question of the unredeemed states had long since been settled.

While Congress was wrangling through its final debates on Saturday, the White House chefs were preparing a magnificent banquet for the leaders of the nation. Ornate carriages began to arrive at the White House, bringing guests for the feast: President-elect Hayes, Vice-President-elect Wheeler, Senator John Sherman, Chief Justice of the Supreme Court Morrison R. Waite, the members of the Cabinet, and many more. The lavish meal, accompanied by many kinds of wine, would be the last blaze of splendor for the Grant Administration.

Just before dinner, Grant called Hayes aside. He pointed out that although Hayes' term of office was due to begin the next day, that day was a Sunday, and it was improper to hold the swearing-in ceremony on the Sabbath. Grant was uneasy about the chances of a Democratic rebellion designed to make Tilden President, and he wanted to take no risks. Instead of waiting until Monday, Grant asked Hayes to take the oath of office now. He could take it again in public on Monday.

Chief Justice Waite presided over the small ceremony. When it was over, they rejoined the others, and from then until midnight that evening, the United States had two Presidents.

On the next day, Sunday, March 4, Tilden remained in New York, against the wishes of those who wanted him to go to Washington and present a dramatic claim for the presidency. "It was impossible to remark any change in his manner," wrote one of Tilden's friends who called on him at this time, "except, perhaps, that he was less absorbed than usual and more interested in current affairs. . . . He has not been so cheerful at any time during the last three years. . . . His notion of being President meant a life of care, responsibility and effort . . . a fearful struggle. When his election was out of the question, he was naturally more sensible of his escape from the giants which he had seen in his path than the honors which might have been his, but were worn by another. . . ."

Though Tilden was clearly relieved that the conflict was over, he showed strain and bitterness, too. His health, never good, had been undermined by the contest, and now he seemed a shrunken old man, his hands trembling with palsy, his limbs twisted by arthritis, his face yellowish, his voice no more than a hoarse whisper. Only the glow of his eyes revealed the still keen mind behind them.

He was generous in defeat. As one of his friends told him, "The whole world knows that your title to the Chief Magistracy of this Country is perfect, and yet you are willing out of pure patriotism to yield your undoubted right." Privately Tilden made a sarcastic pun on his rival's initials, calling him "Returning Board Hayes," but he offered no public challenge to Hayes' inauguration. He seemed almost glad to have lost. To a correspondent he remarked, "I think I can retire to private life with the consciousness that I shall receive from posterity the credit of having been elected to the highest position in the gift of the people without any of the cares and responsibilities of the office."

On Monday, March 5, at noon, Rutherford B. Hayes again took the oath of office as the nineteenth President of the United States.

He had been defeated in the election by more than a quarter of a million votes, and he had acquired a majority of the electoral vote only through an intricate political arrangement. Yet thirty thousand Americans cheered as the bearded man from Ohio rode forth in triumph to take possession of the White House.

11

The Aftermath

President Hayes soon was feeling the great loneliness of the presidency. His was the highest power; but wielding it made him a man apart, the prisoner of his office. In Hayes' case the problems of the presidency were multiplied by the way he had come to the White House. Millions of his fellow citizens regarded him as a usurper. In his own party he was resented by the Stalwarts, who feared that he would succeed in ending their corrupt ways, and was mistrusted by the reformers, who felt he had made an immoral deal with the South. This Republican President had to look toward the southern Democrats to find his strongest support—but even they were interested only in making use of him for their own benefit.

As he settled into office, Hayes realized that his greatest challenge would come from the little band of Republicans who had ruled the nation during the administration of the weak and foolish President Grant. Blaine, Conkling, Morton, Zach Chandler, and the rest would not relinquish power easily. They had opposed him in the struggle for the presidential nomination in the spring of 1876, and he had beaten them; Conkling had tried hard to give the presidency to Tilden, and Hayes had won; now it remained to be seen if Hayes could keep them from dominating him in office.

As he chose his cabinet, Hayes asserted his independence from these cynical, narrow-minded men. John Sherman of Ohio became Secretary of the Treasury—a logical choice, for he had done much to put Hayes in the White House, and was a skilled financier. William M. Evarts of New York, who had argued for Hayes before the Electoral Commission, was named Secretary of State. That infuriated the Radical Republicans, for Evarts had defended President Johnson in his impeachment trial. Carl Schurz, of Missouri, a reformer who had helped to orgnaize the Liberal Republican uprising of 1872, was made Secretary of the Interior. George W. McCrary of Iowa, the man who had devised the Electoral Commission, became Secretary of War. David M. Key of Kentucky, a Democrat and an ex-Confederate, was Hayes' Postmaster General as part of the deal with the South.

These appointments antagonized Conkling, Blaine, and Morton so thoroughly that they tried to block Congressional confirmation of them. Only through southern support did Hayes get his cabinet approved. "Hayes has passed the Republican Party to its worst enemies," Zach Chandler complained. Conkling began to speak of Hayes as "His Fraudulency." Another nickname for him was "Old 8 to 7," a bitter reminder of the votes of the Electoral Commission. By depriving these old guard Republicans of the right to put their friends into high offices, Hayes made his own position extremely precarious. No President could acquire such potent enemies and still hope to control Congress. But with commendable sturdiness Hayes insisted on picking the best available men for the cabinet. Only one really able figure was deliberately overlooked: Benjamin Bristow, the reformer who had exposed so many of the evils of Grantism. Hayes did not dare reward a man so thoroughly detested by so many Republicans, and Bristow faded from public life.

The next task the new President had to face was the solution to the southern problem. As the Southerners pleasantly reminded him, he had made certain promises to them. Now those promises had to be kept.

Of the three southern states that had remained unredeemed in 1876, one, Florida, had already returned to white Democratic control. Although the 1876 election had seen Florida's electoral votes go by manipulation to Hayes, the state had actually had a Democratic majority, and Drew, the Democrat, had become governor. Carpetbaggery was dead there. In Louisiana and South Carolina, though, the gubernatorial elections had ended in confusion and double governments were in operation. The Democrats cliamed that Wade Hampton had been elected Governor of South Carolina and that Francis R. T. Nicholls had been elected Governor of Louisiana. But these states were still occupied by Federal troops sent there by Grant, and the troops had installed two Republican governors: Daniel Chamberlain in South Carolina and S. B. Packard in Louisiana.

The Southerners called upon Hayes to remove the troops, depose Packard and Chamberlain, and recognize Hampton and Nicholls, as pledged at the Wormley's Hotel conference. Now that he was President, however, Hayes found it not so easy to keep his word. For one thing, Packard had received more votes in Louisiana than the Republican presidential electors there, so his claim to the governorship of Louisiana was stronger than Hayes' claim to the presidency of the United States. For another, Hayes would split his own party if he overthrew the two remaining Republican governments in the South. Twelve southern Republican Congressmen announced that they would vote henceforth with the northern Democrats if Packard and Chamberlain were abandoned. If they did, Hayes would be unable to get any legislation approved by Congress.

He hesitated, puzzling over his dilemma. Either way he moved, he would be in trouble. The Southerners were growing impatient. On March 22, 1877, he received a stiff letter from Lucius Q. C. Lamar of Mississippi. Lamar, an important Democrat, had been instrumental in bringing about the Compromise of 1877, as the deal between Hayes and the South was known. He wrote:

"It was understood that you meant to withdraw the troops from South Carolina and Louisiana. . . . Upon that subject we thought you had made up your mind, and indeed you so declared to me. The Packard and Chamberlain governments . . . exist in those states only so long as they were supported by you. . . . If you would achieve what you have begun you must *do* as you *said* you would do."

Hayes could not risk angering the restless Southerners through further delay. He called the two South Carolina governors, Chamberlain and Hampton, to Washington for a conference. Chamberlain seemed to realize he was about to be dumped, and put up little resistance. Hayes met with Hampton and drew from the Democrat an assurance that the rights of Negroes and white Republicans would be respected. On April 3, the President notified Secretary of War McCrary that the threat of "domestic violence" no longer existed in South Carolina, and that the troops could be withdrawn. A week later, the Federal soldiers withdrew from the state capitol building amid the rejoicing of the white population. Chamberlain, no longer protected by their bayonets, turned the capital over to Hampton, and Republican rule ended in South Carolina.

The job was a more delicate one in Louisiana, for if Hayes said Packard had not been elected governor, he was saying that he had not carried the state himself. Since Hayes was safely in the White House, this was not too serious, but he wished to avoid embarrassment. So he appointed a commission of five important Democrats and Republicans to take a second look at the Louisiana gubernatorial election. This was a kind of Electoral Commission in reverse, which would go behind the returns to throw out a Republican who had been elected and install a Democrat who had not been. The commissioners arrived in New Orleans on April 5. Looking over the returns, they discovered that there had been widespread fraud on the part of the Republican returning board, and that the Democrat, Nicholls, had actually been elected governor. (Tilden, too, had carried the state for the Democrats, but these commissioners said not a word about that!) A deal was concocted whereby the Negro Republicans in the pro-Packard Louisiana legislature would agree to take seats in the rival pro-Nicholls legislature. When this was done, the rest of the pro-Packard legislature melted away, and the reorganized Democrat-controlled legislature proclaimed Nicholls as governor. Packard admitted his defeat. On April 24, 1877, the Federal troops filed out of New Orleans to the sound of gaily clanging bells.

Reconstruction was dead. The carpetbaggers were through. The South now was ruled by white Democrats everywhere. President Hayes was hailed by some as "the greatest Southerner of the day."

He tried to soften the blow for the dethroned carpetbaggers by finding government jobs for them. In particular, those southern Republicans who had taken part in his own dubious election were well rewarded. All the members of the Louisiana returning board were given highly paid jobs in the United States Treasury Department. Sixteen officials on the staff of the returning board, twenty-seven election supervisors, the seven Republican electors, and thirteen assorted members of Louisiana's outgoing Republican government also got Federal jobs. Twenty election officials of Florida were given Federal appointments, including the entire returning board. Louisiana's ex-Governor Packard was soothed with the job of United States Consul in Liverpool, where he was entitled to collect fees amounting to more than the salary of President Hayes. Kellogg, his predecessor, who had signed the Hayes electoral certificate from Louisiana, was allowed to enter the United States Senate as a Republican despite the general knowledge that his election was corrupt. Stearns, the defeated Republican Governor of Florida, got a good job for signing the Hayes certificate there. Numerous South Carolina Republicans received high appointments. The political payoff also extended to the "visiting statesmen" who had guided the doings of the returning boards. One was made a senator, one was appointed Governor of the Territory of New Mexico, three became ambassadors to European countries.

Not only jobless Republicans benefited from Hayes' election. He took good care to strengthen his position in the South by naming Democrats to local offices. Such cities as Louisville, Memphis, and St. Petersburg were turned over to Democratic postmasters. Over the anguished cries of Republican leaders, Hayes gave jobs to Democrats in every southern state. In his first five months in office, one out of every three jobs in the South filled by presidential appointment went to a Democrat.

The South was content with the new President. When Hayes toured the South in the fall of 1877, happy onlookers cheered him enthusiastically. Only twelve years before, a Southerner had assassinated a Republican President; it was strange to see a Republican now traveling through a delighted South with an ex-Confederate, Governor Wade Hampton, riding beside him.

In the North, though, Hayes found himself in deepening political trouble. He was a President without a party, cut off from Republican support by the enmity of the Stalwarts. His attempt to reform the government was exhausting and difficult, for he had to fight Republicans every step of the way. His biggest battle for reform came over the cleanup of the New York Customshouse. Chester Alan Arthur, the Collector of Customs, was an important Conkling lieutenant and had acquired great wealth and political power through his control of the Customshouse. When an investigation in the summer of 1877 revealed the looseness and inefficiency of Arthur's office, Hayes dismissed him and appointed a new Collector. Conkling saw to it that the Senate voted, 31 to 25, against approving the new appointment.

"I am right," Hayes said, "and shall not give up the contest." After Congress adjourned he removed Arthur anyway, and put his own man in. When the next session of Congress opened, Secretary of the Treasury John Sherman handled his old Senate colleagues so cleverly that the appointment was allowed to stand, preventing the embarrassment of the President. But this was virtually the only important political victory Hayes enjoyed.

His administration was further marred in the summer of 1877 by labor rioting. The Baltimore & Ohio Railroad cut the wages of its employees by 10 percent. A strike followed, and when a rally in support of the strikers got out of hand, the Maryland militia fired into the crowd and killed twelve people. The strike spread to Pittsburgh, where fifty-seven strikers and soldiers were killed, and millions of dollars of damage was done. President Hayes was forced to call out Federal troops and send them into Maryland, West Virginia, Pennsylvania, Illinois, and Missouri to restore order. The man who had won the White House by pledging to withdraw Federal soldiers from the South found himself imposing military rule on the North.

And so he moved on to the end of his controversial four years in office. Harassed by his own party, eventually deserted by most of the Democrats as well, he became a sorrowful, isolated figure, a President who meant well but who failed to gain support for any of his projects. Before he became President, Hayes had said that he planned to serve only one term. He did not necessarily mean it, since he had said the same thing when becoming Governor of Ohio, and had gone on to serve three times. His "one-term" pledge became a convenient way of saving face as his unhappy presidency came to its close. If he had tried to run again,

Hayes would have been denied the nomination by his Republican enemies—the ultimate humiliation for a President. Instead, clinging to his pledge, he left office gracefully and returned to Ohio. His friend and fellow Ohioan, James A. Garfield, was nominated by the Republicans and elected to the high office in 1880, only to fall victim to an assassin's bullet a year later. The man who became President then was the handsome, lighthearted former Collector of Customs—Chester Alan Arthur.

When Hayes left the White House on March 4, 1881, one cruel comment became a popular joke: "Mr. Hayes came in by a majority of one and goes out by unanimous consent." No one could have been more amused by this than Samuel J. Tilden.

For four years, Tilden had quietly looked upon himself as the rightful but deposed President of the United States. His first public statement on the subject had come on June 13, 1877, when he was the guest of honor at a political dinner in New York. Speaking in a voice so faint it could scarcely be heard, he said:

"Everybody know that, after the recent election, the men who were elected by the people as President and Vice-President were counted out; and the men who were not elected were counted in and seated. If my voice could reach throughout our country and be heard in its remotest hamlet, I would say: Be of good cheer. The Republic will live. The institutions of our fathers are not to expire in shame. The sovereignty of the people shall be rescued from this peril and re-established."

Four months later he sounded a more vigorous note. Returning from a summer in Europe, Tilden delivered an improvised speech at his home a day after his arrival. He spoke of "the greatest political crime of our history, by which the result of the presidential election of 1876 was set aside and reversed." Someone in the audience yelled, "We know you got robbed!" and Tilden replied,

"I did not get robbed. The people got robbed . . . robbed of the dearest rights of American citizens." Then he said:

"Young men! . . . we who have guarded the sacred traditions of our free government will soon leave that work to you. . . . Whether our institutions shall be preserved . . . will depend on you. Will you accomplish that duty, and mark these wrongdoers of 1876 with the indignation of a betrayed, wronged, and sacrificed people? . . . I swear in the presence of you all, and I call upon you to bear witness to the oath, to watch, during the remainder of my life, over the rights of the citizens of our country with a jealous care. Such a usurpation must never occur again."

During 1877 and 1878 it was assumed by most Americans, both Republicans and Democrats, that Tilden would run for President again in 1880, would win again, and this time would be allowed to take office. The shame and guilt in the nation over the stolen election was great, and some atonement to Tilden was thought necessary. In the spring of 1878 the House of Representatives appointed a committee to investigate the disputed election, and the work of this committee served to convince most citizens that Tilden had indeed been the winner.

Suppressed details of the scandal came into the open. It now was clear that Republican bribery had bought the votes of the returning board. Bribe offers from Tilden's men were revealed too, but all of these had been vetoed by the candidate; if he had been willing to pay the price, he would have been President. Some newspapers demanded that Hayes be ejected from the White House in midterm and Tilden put into office, but this, of course, was never seriously considered in Congress, and would have been opposed by Tilden.

As the 1880 nominating convention approached, though, practical politics interfered with the second Tilden candidacy. He was old and feeble now; even though the nation owed him the presidency, he would not have been strong enough to survive the burdens of office. And many Democratic politicians, feeling he had not fought hard enough for his rights in 1876, wanted the nomination to go to a more vigorous man. Tilden himself believed he could be elected, and he was probably right. But he took a characteristically complicated attitude toward the nomination. On June 18, 1880, the eve of the Democratic convention, he sent a long letter to the delegates, beginning with a summary of the events by which he was "elected to the presidency" and then "counted out." He concluded by saying that the task of the highest office "is now, I fear, beyond my strength," and offered "unfeigned thanks for the honors bestowed upon me."

To most delegates this seemed like the withdrawal statement of a tired old man who did not want to run. They took it at face value and gave the nomination to General Winfield Scott Hancock. However, it appears that Tilden really did want the nomination, but had not wished to seem too eager for it, and had hoped the convention would thrust it upon him over his seeming reluctance.

He was past all such subtleties by 1884. Even though he was now seventy years old—older than any man ever elected to the presidency at that time—he still had friends who wished to see him in the White House, and the nomination and election would have been his for the asking. This time he knew his life was nearly over, and he plainly declined the honor, saying, "I but submit to the will of God in deeming my public career forever closed." The Governor of New York, Grover Cleveland, was nominated, and ended a quarter of a century of Republican rule at last when he was elected to the presidency that fall. With a Democratic President in office, Tilden served as an elder statesman, advising Cleveland during his early months as Chief Executive and energetically spurring him to take active measures for reform. When death came to Tilden in 1886, the whole nation mourned the departed leader. Flags flew at half staff for the man who had been elected President but who had not been allowed to serve. John Greenleaf Whittier produced the funeral ode:

> Once more, O all-adjusting Death!
> The Nation's Pantheon opens wide;
> Once more a common sorrow saith
> A strong, wise man has died.

> Ambitious, cautious, yet the man
> To strike down a fraud with resolute hand;
> A patriot, if a partisan,
> He loved his native land.

Hayes lived on in Ohio retirement, going over his scrapbooks, recollecting past battles, and, as ever, devouring books of history and philosophy for "mental improvement—for information—to keep the faculties alert and alive." His qualms over the 1876 election never left him, but he rarely displayed signs that he felt guilty or embarrassed. He had tried to be a good President, he had done his best, and if he had failed, it was because stubborn, greedy men had opposed him. His sturdy, bearded figure became a familiar sight now in times of national grief. Deeply shaken, he rode in the funeral procession of his martyred successor, President Garfield, in 1881. Four years later, with ex-President Arthur beside him, Hayes took part in the final ceremonies for Ulysses S. Grant. Then, in 1886, it was Arthur who went to the grave, and Hayes rode in the carriage with President Cleveland at the funeral. The men of Hayes' world were passing. His closing years were clouded, too, by attacks on the legitimacy of his presidency. Alone among the men who had lived in the White House, Hayes had come to power improperly, and every retelling of the story of 1876 wounded him.

When he died on January 17, 1893, in his seventy-first year, he was laid to rest with the magnificence befitting a true President. Troops paraded; muffled drums were beat; President Cleveland stood with head bared under the gray, wintry Ohio sky. The entire Ohio legislature was there, and so was Governor William McKinley, himself marked for the White House and tragedy. Hayes had come to prominence in the year the nation celebrated its hundredth birthday at the Centennial Exposition in Philadelphia; he left the world in the year of another grand fair, this one in Chicago, honoring the 400th anniversary of Columbus' voyage to the New World.

And so it was finished. The men of 1876 were gone; the scandal faded into history, and most Americans forgot that there was a time when one man had won the presidency and another had taken the White House.

What were the effects of that event? How was history changed? Did it matter, really, whether Hayes or Tilden had been sworn in?

It mattered. Hayes was the President of reconciliation. He buried the bloody shirt, forgave the South for its rebellion, and drew the nation together after the decades of bitterness. As a Republican, as a Civil War veteran who had been wounded to save the Union, Hayes could do this. Tilden could not. As a Democrat, as a man with no war record, he would not have been in a strong enough position. Whatever he did to help the South would have been regarded in the North as treason. Hayes was bitterly enough blamed for his kindly treatment of the South, but at least he could not be accused of secret Confederate leanings. He saved the nation from the danger of continued strife between North and South.

Tilden saved the nation too, great patriot that he was. If he had tried to claim by force what the people wished him to have, war might have resulted. Only a man of towering character could have turned his back on the presidency so that no bloodshed would be caused. He stood aside voluntarily. That was the measure of his greatness.

The nation gained because Hayes put an end to the evils of Radical Reconstruction. Whether he did it freely or because he had made a political deal is beside the point; he cast the carpet-baggers down, and made the Southerners their own masters again. In other ways, though, the 1876 election worked great harm.

Most obvious is the harm done to democracy. The vote of the people was ignored. This was something that should never have happened, and must never happen again.

The country was deprived of the services of Samuel J. Tilden—a great reformer, a great administrator. Whether Tilden would have been able to function effectively as President in the tense United States of 1877–80 we can never know; but he should have had the chance.

The crime of 1876 had a powerful effect on future generations, too. It robbed the American Negro of his voice in political life, and brought about injustices that are only now being corrected. In a way, it called back and cancelled the accomplishments of the Civil War.

Men had fought and died to free the slaves. After the war, the Republicans had emerged as the champions of the Negro. They went too far, though, committing the excesses of Reconstruction, forcing the defeated southern whites to submit to the rule of their own ex-slaves. Placing illiterate Negroes into positions of power created hatred among the whites that still has not died away. But the storms of Reconstruction eventually brought about something even worse: the recapture by the whites of a dominant position, and the loss of all civil rights by the Negroes.

This would have happened eventually even if Tilden had won, since all but three southern states had been redeemed by 1876. But the events of that year finished the job. The troops were taken out of the South; the white Democrats were given control; and the Republicans, in their eagerness to have the White House, abandoned the Negroes to their fate. The deal between Hayes and the South left the whites free to do as they pleased with their black neighbors, confident that there would be no Federal interference. As the liberal *Nation* said sadly, "The Negro will disappear from the field of national politics. Henceforth the nation, as a nation, will have nothing more to do with him." And the New York *Tribune* said farewell to the era of Negro power in the South with a typical example of the thinking of the times. The Negroes, said the *Tribune,* "after ample opportunity to develop their own latent capacities," had merely proved that "as a race they are idle, ignorant, and vicious."

Governor Wade Hampton of South Carolina did his best to work for Negro rights, as he had promised when President Hayes put him in office. He gave the Negroes better schools, honest justice, protection from white racists, and a number of state jobs. As his reward, he was overthrown and defeated by the white people of his state.

Night descended once more for the Negro of the South. He lost the right to vote, to hold office, to exercise the ordinary privileges of any citizen. The restored white rulers were determined to make up for the years when Negroes had enjoyed the favor of the carpetbaggers. The southern states prohibited Negroes from going to the same schools as whites, from entering churches or theaters used by whites, from eating at the same restaurants. The Negro was no longer a slave, but otherwise he was reduced to second-class citizenship. Negroes who protested were beaten or killed. And the Republican Party, once the great defender of the Negro, did nothing. This was the worst heritage of the Compromise of 1877. It broke the alliance between Republicans and Negroes that had come out of the Civil War, and condemned black Americans to eighty more years of misery before the national government once again began to fight for the rights of these oppressed people.

There had never been an election like that of 1876 in American history before. There has never been one since, although the electoral system has not greatly changed, and an extremely close election might well have the same chaotic outcome. The Hayes-Tilden contest produced a sorry spectacle. The forces that controlled it are still with us: the bitterness between white man and black, the hunger for power, the willingness to betray high ideals when high office is at stake. Probably we will be spared the turmoil and the agony of a disputed electoral count again, but the possibility remains alive. And if it comes to pass, the entire world will watch in fear and wonder as the giant of democracy struggles once more to choose its leader.

For Further Information

Barnard, Harry. *Rutherford B. Hayes and His America.* Bobbs-Merrill, 1954.

Burnham, W. D. *Presidential Ballots, 1836–1892.* Johns Hopkins Press, 1955.

Butterfield, Roger. *The American Past.* Simon & Schuster, 1965.

Bryce, James. *The American Commonwealth.* Macmillan, 1896.

Dunning, William A. *Reconstruction, Political and Economic, 1865–1877.* Harper Torchbooks, 1962.

Eaton, Herbert. *Presidential Timber: A History of Nominating Conventions, 1868–1960.* The Free Press of Glencoe, 1964.

Eckenrode, H. J. *Rutherford B. Hayes, Statesman of Reunion.* Dodd, Mead, 1930.

Flick, Alexander C. *Samuel Jones Tilden, A Study in Political Sagacity.* Kennikat Press, 1963.

Haworth, P. L. *The Hayes-Tilden Disputed Presidential Election of 1876.* Burroues, 1906.

Hewitt, A. S. "Secret History of the Disputed Election, 1876–1877." In *Selected Writings,* edited by Allan Nevin. Columbia University Press, 1937.

Josephson, Matthew. *The Politicos.* Harcourt, Brace, 1938.

Judah, Charles and Smith, George Winston. *The Unchosen.* Coward-McCann, 1962.

Robinson, Lloyd. *The Hopefuls: Ten Presidential Campaigns.* Doubleday, 1966.

Roseboom, Eugene H. *A History of Presidential Elections.* Macmillan, 1957.

Sherman, John. *Recollections.* Werner, 1895.

Stampp, Kenneth M. *The Era of Reconstruction 1865–1877.* Knopf, 1965.

Tugwell, Rexford G. *How They Became President.* Simon & Schuster, 1964.

Wilmerding, Lucius, Jr. *The Electoral College.* Rutgers University Press, 1958.

Woodward, C. Vann. *Reunion & Reaction.* Doubleday Anchor Books, 1956.

Index

Abbott, Josiah, 161
Adams, Charles Francis, 192
Adams, Henry, 63
Adams, John, 13
Adams, John Quincy, 145
Allen, William, 67
Ames, General Adelbert, 42–43
Andersonville (prison camp),
    53–54, 110
Arthur, Chester Alan, 13, 63,
    204–5, 206, 209
Atlantic Monthly, 181

Babcock, Orville, 44
Baltimore & Ohio Railroad, 205
Barlow, Francis, 136
Baxter, Governor Elisha, 29–30
Bayard, Thomas F., 67, 161
Belknap, William W., 44–45
Birchard, Sardis, 71, 72, 73, 77,
    78
Blackburn, Joseph C., 188
"Black Laws," 20, 21, 22
Blaine, James G., 46–48, 49, 55,
    58, 59, 60, 61, 62, 63, 77, 79,
    106, 108, 159, 199
    presidential candidate, 46–48,
    49, 55, 58, 59, 60, 61, 62, 63
    Union Pacific scandal, 54

"Bloody shirt," 32, 46, 53, 77–78,
    105, 106, 174–75, 180, 210
Bogy, Lewis V., 168
Booth, John Wilkes, 18
Boynton, General Henry Van
    Ness, 173
Bradley Joseph P., 161–62,
    166–68, 169–70, 191–92
Bristow, Benjamin, 44, 63, 200
    candidate, 48, 55, 56, 58, 59,
    60, 61, 62
    reformer, 44
    See also Whiskey Ring
Brodhead, James O., 67
Brooks, Joseph, 30
Buchanan, James, 13
Bureau of Correspondence, 101
Burke, E. A, 183
Burns, A. M., 57
Burr, Aaron, 145

Canal Ring, 94, 109
Carpetbaggers, 23–25, 26, 27, 29,
    30, 32–33, 36, 38, 42, 46, 48,
    59, 66, 94, 104–5, 138, 149,
    172, 174, 183–84, 201, 203,
    211
    in the 1876 election, 104, 105,
    114, 115, 119, 120, 122, 123,
    134–35, 137–40

Centennial Exposition, 68, 69,
	100, 111, 210
Central Pacific Railroad, 174
Chamberlain, Daniel H., 115–16,
	121, 133, 201–2
Chandler, William E, 121–22,
	123, 135, 140, 159
Chandler, Zachariah, 106–8, 110,
	121, 123–25, 135, 199–200
"Cheap money," 38–40, 48, 49,
	50, 59, 66
	See also "Greenbacks"; Panic
	of 1873
Chicago *Tribune,* 20, 160
Cincinnati *Enquirer,* 176, 191–92
Civil rights (Negro), 19, 21,
	23–24, 31–32, 59, 78, 88,
	102–3, 105–6, 108, 183–84,
	202, 210–13
	See also Suffrage (Negro)
Civil War, 14, 17, 18, 19, 20, 25,
	47, 48, 59, 66, 74–76, 79,
	86–88, 104, 108, 110, 117,
	120, 148–49, 173–74, 210
Clay, Henry, 145
Cleveland, Grover, 208, 209
Clifford, Nathan, 161
Comley, General James, 180, 181
Committee on Electoral Count,
	151, 153, 154, 157–58, 159
Compromise of 1877, 15, 150,
	175, 177, 193, 201–2, 212
	See also Wormley's Hotel
Conkling, Roscoe, 47, 49, 50, 53,
	56, 59, 60, 61, 62, 63, 64, 70,
	93, 108, 110, 131, 151, 159,
	199, 205
Constitution of the United States,

14, 21, 74, 86, 106, 108, 113,
	127, 131, 132, 143–44, 147,
	154
Cooke, Jay, 29
Cooper, Peter, 98
Cooper Institute, 92
Copperheads, 86, 87, 180
Council for Political Reform, 91
	See also Tweed Ring
Crawford, William, 145
Cronin, E. A., 128

Dana, Charles A., 151
Davis, David, 158, 160, 193
Davis, Jefferson, 53
Democratic convention of 1876,
	66–68, 108
Democratic party, 35
Drew, Governor G. F., 136, 137,
	165, 201

Edmunds, George, 161
Eisenhower, Dwight D., 13
Electoral College, 14
Electoral Commission, 110,
	154–61, 163–72, 176–77,
	178–80, 183, 185, 187, 189
	Florida ruling, 164–69
	Louisiana ruling, 169–70
	Oregon ruling, 168, 178–80
	South Carolina ruling, 168, 195
Electoral system, 14, 15–16, 112,
	127, 132, 134, 141–47, 154,
	180, 197, 200, 212–13
Evarts, William H., 183, 200

Fairchild, Charles S., 93
Ferry, Thomas W., 43, 144,
	163–64, 185–86, 188, 189

Field, David Dudley, 165
Field, Stephen J., 161
Fifteenth Amendment, 106
Fifth Avenue Hotel, 121
Filibuster, 171–72, 178–80,
    181–82, 183, 186–89, 193
Fillmore, Millard, 13
Flagg, Azariah C., 85
Ford's Theater, 18
Foster, Charles, 179, 183
Fourteenth Amendment, 21, 22,
    29, 106
Frelinghuysen, Frederick, 161

Garfield, James A., 13, 129, 147,
    150, 159, 161, 179, 183, 206,
    209
Garland, Augustus H., 149
Garvey, Mr. (plasterer), 90
Gibson, A. M., 151
Gould, Jay, 37
Grant, Ulysses S., 13, 14, 25–28,
    29, 30–31, 33, 37–38,
    39–40, 42, 43, 44–46, 47,
    56, 64, 69, 78, 89, 94, 116,
    125, 145, 171, 179, 191, 195,
    199, 200, 201, 209
    character, 25–27, 38, 45, 69
    corruption, 25–27, 29, 37, 42,
    43–45, 46, 47, 48, 94, 191
    in the election of 1876, 53, 116,
    129–30, 133, 141, 150, 154,
    155, 161
    See also Panic of 1873
Greeley, Horace, 27–28, 109, 111
"Greenbacks," 39–40, 66, 67
    See also "Cheap money";
    Panic of 1873

Gresham, Walter, 116
Grover, Governor L. F., 127–28

Half-Breeds, 47
Hampton, Wade, 102, 116, 133,
    183, 201–2, 204, 212
Hancock, General Winfield Scott,
    50, 67, 208
Harlan, John, 60, 61, 62
Harper's Weekly, 91
Harrison, Benjamin, 13, 108
Harrison, William Henry, 72, 82
Hartranft, Governor John F.,
    48–49, 60, 61, 62
Harvard University, 72
Hayes, Rutherford B.
    in Civil War, 16, 74–77, 78, 88
    compromise with the South,
    134, 150, 172–74, 176–78,
    179–81, 182–84, 185, 187,
    194–95, 200–203, 211–12
    election of 1876, 14, 17–18, 49,
    55–59, 68, 69–70, 71, 94, 97,
    101–2, 103, 104–8, 110–11,
    112–14, 115, 116–42, 143,
    144, 145, 148–52, 153–54,
    156, 158, 161–62, 189
    Electoral Commission, 154,
    161, 164–68, 170, 171–72,
    178, 185, 187
    electoral count, 163–66,
    168–69, 176–77, 178, 182,
    185–89
    ends Reconstruction, 18,
    202–5, 210
    life, 71–79
    personality, 16, 56, 58, 63, 70,
    71, 73, 95, 111, 190

Hayes, Rutherford B. (*cont.*)
  in politics, 16, 56–57, 58, 72,
    73–74, 75–79
  as President, 189–92, 194, 195,
    196–206, 207
  Republican convention, 48–49,
    56, 58–63
  retirement, 209–10
Hayes, Webb, 161
Hendricks, Thomas A., 32, 50, 66,
    67, 101, 114, 118, 141, 148
Hewitt, Abram S., 98, 101, 107,
    120, 127–28, 129, 140,
    147–48, 150, 151–52,
    154–56, 160, 161, 166, 182,
    185, 189, 193–94
*History of the Abolition of the
  Slave Trade* (Clarkson), 74
Hoar, George, 161
Holman, William S., 175
Hunton, Eppa, 161

Ingersoll, Colonel Robert G., 60,
    108–9

Jackson, Andrew, 35, 40, 45,
    80–81, 145
Jefferson, Thomas, 13, 45, 68, 145
Jewel, Marshall, 49, 59–60, 61
Johnson, Andrew, 18–20, 22, 23,
    25, 76, 88, 158
  impeachment, 25
  "Restoration" program, 19–20,
    88
Johnston, General Joseph E., 177

Kasson, J. A., 175
Kellar, Colonel Andrew J.,
    172–73

Kellogg, Governor William P., 28,
    30, 141, 169–70, 203
Kelly, John, 66–67
Kennedy, John F., 13
Kenyon College, 72
Kernan, Francis, 66
Kerr, Michael C., 43, 163
Key, David M., 149, 177, 200
Know-Nothings, 85
Ku Klux Klan, 25, 26, 30, 32
  See also Rifle clubs; White
    League

Lamar, Lucius Q. C., 201
"Lame ducks," 40
Levy, William M., 187
Liberal Republicans, 26, 29, 38,
    54–55, 78, 200
Lincoln, Abraham, 13, 17–18, 19,
    36, 45–46, 56, 76, 87, 88,
    104, 109, 158
Literary Bureau, 99, 111
  See also Newspaper Popularity
    Bureau

McCrary, George W., 150, 200,
    202
McEnery, John, 27–28, 30, 141,
    169
McKinley, William, 75, 210
Madison, James, 13, 45, 68
Magone, Dan, 120
Marble, Manton, 135–36
Marcy, Governor William L.,
    81–82, 94
Memphis *Avalanche,* 172
Mexican War, 84
Miller, Samuel F., 161

Mills, Roger Q., 188
Monroe, James, 13, 45
Morgan, J. P., 37
Morton, Oliver P., 39, 48, 56, 59,
    60, 61, 62, 108, 151, 154,
    159, 161, 199–200

Nashville *Banner,* 174
Nast, Tom, 91
Nation, The, 107, 110, 116, 212
National Republican, 180
New Orleans *Times,* 149, 174–75
Newspaper Popularity Bureau, 65,
    99
    See also Literary Bureau
New York *Evening Post,* 119
New York *Herald,* 119–20, 125
New York *Sun,* 151, 167, 192
New York *Times,* 91, 110, 111,
    120, 122, 124, 126, 156
New York *Tribune,* 27, 59,
    119–21, 212
New York University, 82
New York *World,* 63, 124
Nicholls, Francis, 183, 201–3
Northern Pacific Railroad, 29
Noyes, General Edward F., 58–59,
    59, 129

Ohio State Journal, 125, 180, 182

Packard, S. B., 201–3
Panic of 1873, 29, 31, 32, 38, 49,
    66, 106, 149, 174
    See also "Cheep money";
    "Greenbacks"
Parker, Governor Joel, 50, 66
Payne, Henry B., 151, 161

Pelton, W. T., 135, 140, 170
"People's Indignation
    Convention," 148
Pierce, Franklin, 13
Presidential Courts, The (Tilden),
    152–53
Pulitzer, Joseph, 63, 152–53

Race riots, 22, 42, 104, 115–16
Radical Republicans, 19, 21–23,
    24, 25, 27, 32–33, 41, 47, 48,
    76, 87, 89, 102, 106, 158,
    161, 174, 175, 181, 211
    See also Reconstruction
Randall, Samuel J., 163, 178–79,
    181, 182, 186–87, 189,
    192–93
Reconstruction, 18–25, 26,
    32–33, 37, 38, 46, 76–77, 89,
    94, 122, 174, 211
    See also Radical Republicans
Reconstruction Act, 22, 88
Redeemers, 173
Redemption, 26, 27–29, 103, 115,
    118, 119–20, 133–34, 182,
    195, 201, 211
    Mississippi, 42–43
Reid, John C., 119–23, 124
Republican convention of 1876,
    56, 58–62
Republican Party, 17, 36, 74
"Returning boards," 123, 128–30,
    132–33, 135–37, 166, 170,
    204, 207
    Florida, 123, 124, 135–37,
    165–66, 203
    Louisiana, 123, 124, 137,
    139–41, 169, 203–4
    South Carolina, 130, 141, 143

Rifle clubs, 42, 104, 115–16
Roberts, Colonel W. H., 149
Robeson, George M., 26
Rockefeller, John D., 37, 101
Roosevelt, Franklin Delano, 13

Scalawags, 23, 26, 42, 48, 105,
    135
Schurz, Carl, 200
Scott, Tom, 190
Secret History (Hewitt), 193
Seymour, Horatio, 25, 64, 88–89,
    93
Sherman, John, 40, 57–58, 64,
    108, 129, 130, 132, 138–39,
    151, 154, 159, 169, 182, 183,
    191, 195, 199–200, 205
Sherman, General William
    Tecumseh, 130, 137, 177,
    191
Slavery, 17, 18–19, 36, 72–73, 74,
    79, 83–84, 88, 106, 148, 172,
    211, 212
Smith, William Henry, 172
Speaker's Bureau, 100
Springfield *Republican,* 64
Stalwarts, 27, 29, 41, 43, 47, 48,
    59–60, 107, 199, 204
Sterns, Governor M. L., 137, 165,
    204
Stevens, John G., 166, 167
Stevens, Thaddeus, 18–19, 20, 22,
    76
Strong, William, 161
Suffrage (Negro), 21, 22–24,
    25–26, 27, 32, 37, 43, 78, 86,
    105–6, 213
  in 1876 election, 102–3,

    113–14, 115, 118, 125–26,
    130, 132, 137, 138–39

Tammany Hall, 66–67, 68, 89–93
Taylor, Zachary, 13
Texas Pacific Railroad, 167
Thirteenth Amendment, 106
Tilden, Samuel J., 13–15
  and the Civil War, 87–88
  Democratic convention, 49–51,
    64, 65–68
  election of 1876, 93–95,
    97–105, 118–20, 122–24,
    125–30
  Electoral Commission, 151–60,
    163–72
  electoral count, 135–37, 139,
    140–42, 145–48, 178–79,
    185–89
  electoral loss, reaction to,
    192–94
  life, 79–89, 206–9
  personality, 16, 65, 93–95,
    175–76
  in politics, 49–51, 83–87
  slanders against, 109–12
  and Boss Tweed, 64–65, 89–93
Truman, Harry, 13

Union Pacific Railroad, 54, 174
Union Party, 18–19, 87

Van Buren, Martin, 50, 80–81, 82
Vanderbilt, Cornelius, 37, 101
Vicksburg *Herald,* 174

Waite, Morrison R. 155, 195
War Democrats, 87, 110
Warmoth, Henry C., 27

Washington, George, 13, 45, 68
Washington *Union,* 191
Watterson, Henry, 66, 129,
   139–40, 48, 183–84
Watts, J. W., 127–28, 180
Webb, Lucy Ware, 73
Weed, Smith M., 133
Wells, J. M., 137, 140
Wheeler, William A., 62, 63, 118,
   189, 195

Whig Party, 35–36, 72, 73–74,
   82, 83, 106, 173
Whiskey Ring, 44, 55
White League, 30
"White Men's Clubs," 103
Whittier, John Greenleaf, 209
Wilson, Henry, 43
Wormley's Hotel, 183–84, 187,
   201

Yale University, 81